N.S. KHRUSHCHEV: THE 'SECRET' SPEECH

THE 'SECRET' SPEECH

delivered to the closed session of the Twentieth Congress of the Communist Party of the Soviet Union

by

Nikita Sergeyevich Khrushchev

with an introduction by

Zhores A. Medvedev and Roy A. Medvedev

published for the
Bertrand Russell Peace Foundation
by
Spokesman Books

The 'Secret' Speech of Nikita
Khrushchev.
Published on June 4th, 1976,
to mark the 20th anniversary of
its world-wide publication.

Published in 1976 for the
Bertrand Russell Peace Foundation Ltd.
Bertrand Russell House,
Gamble Street, Nottingham by
Spokesman Books.
Printed by the Russell Press Ltd.,
Nottingham.

Copyright
　Introduction © Zhores A. Medvedev
　and Roy A. Medvedev 1976
　Translation © Tamara Deutscher 1976.
　Notes © Spokesman Books 1976.

Contents

Acknowledgements — page 6

1: **Introduction**
   by Zhores A. Medvedev and Roy A. Medvedev — page 9

2: **The 'Secret' Speech**
   delivered by N.S. Khrushchev to the closed session of the 20th Congress of the C.P.S.U. — page 19

   Explanatory Notes to the 'Secret' Speech — page 81

3: **Documents circulated as an addendum to N.S. Khrushchev's Secret Speech** — page 89

4: **A Resolution of the Central Committee of the C.P.S.U.** — page 113

ACKNOWLEDGEMENTS

On June 4 1956 the State Department for Foreign Affairs of the United States Government released the text of a statement made by N.S. Khrushchev, February 24-25 1956, to a special closed session of the Twentieth Congress of the Communist Party of the Soviet Union. Eighteen documents which had been circulated with that statement were also released.

This volume contains all these materials, together with an introduction by Zhores and Roy Medvedev, which explains the immediate background to Khrushchev's statement, and how it became public knowledge in the USSR. This introduction was translated from the Russian by Tamara Deutscher. The explanatory notes to the main text were prepared by Ken Coates.

The book also includes a resolution of the Central Committee of the CPSU on the overcoming of the consequences of the cult of personality.

In view of the continuing importance of these documents for the world-wide communist and socialist movements, the Bertrand Russell Peace Foundation resolved to mark the 20th anniversary of their first appearance with this and other publications by the distinguished Soviet historian, Roy Medvedev.

In this short introduction Zhores and Roy Medvedev summarise the events leading up to, and immediately resulting from, Nikita Khrushchev's epoch-making statement.

A definitive account of the history of Stalinism, Let History Judge, *by Roy Medvedev, is available from Spokesman Books as a companion volume to this one, in paperback format.*

Introduction
by Zhores A. Medvedev and Roy A. Medvedev

Introduction

THE HISTORICAL IMPORTANCE OF KHRUSHCHEV'S SPEECH AT THE TWENTIETH CONGRESS OF THE CPSU

The twenty-fifth Congress of the Communist Party of the Soviet Union opened in Moscow on 24 February 1976. This was a significant date, an anniversary; but none of the participants of the Congress openly mentioned this fact, though many of them remembered in what circumstances, two decades before, on 24 February 1956, the Twentieth Congress, the first after Stalin's death, was officially declared closed. That Congress was in session for nearly ten days, from 14 to 24 February, and ended after the election of the new Plenum of the Central Committee of the CPSU.

Traditionally, the Plenum of the Central Committee begins by electing the First Secretary of the Party, who then proposes for election the members of the new Presidium. On 24 February 1956 Nikita S. Khrushchev became the First Secretary. For a very short spell of a few hours, before tne new Presidium is formed, the First Secretary has practically unlimited powers. The whole scenario for the election of the new Presidium as well as the list of its members has been decided earlier, before the beginning of the Congress. The First Secretary's duty is to wind up proceedings according to the previously prepared plan.

However, quite unexpectedly, Khrushchev announced that the Congress would continue in a fresh closed session, from which foreign delegations and foreign guests were to be excluded. It was nearly midnight, but Khrushchev could not put off the session till the next day as this might have upset his plans: many delegates were to leave Moscow on the morning of 25 February and return to their respective regions. A special summons — to gather in the Kremlin for a closed night session of the Congress — was issued to all delegates. Most of them were staying in hotels in the vicinity: so within

25 or 30 minutes the hall of the Congress was nearly full. Nikita S. Khrushchev stepped onto the podium greeted by applause and, without announcing any agenda for the closed session, began his four-hour long speech, which by now has entered history, about Stalin's crimes towards the Party and the whole nation.

The delegates listened to Khrushchev in shock and silence, only from time to time one could hear expressions of astonishment and indignation. There was no discussion after the speech, and in the early hours of the morning, on 25 February, the Twentieth Congress of the CPSU was brought to a close for the second time. It was precisely this unforeseen night session with its unannounced speech about the iniquities committed in the period of the "cult of personality" that became the genuine Twentieth Congress which entered history and changed the course of the international communist movement.

We shall not repeat here the burden of Khrushchev's speech which is reproduced in full as the main content of this volume.

The speech could not, of course, have been kept secret; and Khrushchev himself did not even try to keep it secret. A few days later, in accordance with the decision of the new Secretariat of the Central Committee dominated by Khrushchev's nominees, the text of the speech was printed and despatched to regional Party Committees so that the activists should become acquainted with it. Those responsible party workers, whose names were on the official register, were called into the offices and handed a red booklet containing Khrushchev's speech, which was to be read on the spot. The booklet could not be taken out of the room, and there was always an instructor present to see that the readers did not make any excerpts. Two weeks later the booklets were also sent to district committees, to be read, again in confidence, by activists at the district level. After that all registered party members were called into the offices of the district committees and the text was distributed in the party cells of factories, of scientific institutes and other large party organizations. The process of the reading of the "secret" speech was acquiring the character of a chain reaction. At the end of March 1956 there followed a new directive: Khrushchev's speech was to be read at meetings in all establishments, in factories, in kolkhozes, at universities, in educational institutions, and even in the upper forms of schools to pupils over 14-15 years old. Everybody was to be acquainted with it, party members as well as non-party citizens. In a short time the "secret" speech, delivered at the "closed" session of the Congress, became known to tens of millions of people, to the majority of the adult population of the Soviet Union. Copies of the speech were sent to the leaderships of all Communist Parties abroad, and the foreign press soon got hold of the text. Although it was never actually published in the Soviet Union, beyond its frontiers the speech was translated into all the main languages including Russian.

When one analyses Khrushchev's speech now, it becomes obvious that it was prepared with a certain haste, without careful selection and analysis of the material. It was very far from containing all the grave truths about Stalin's offences; supplementary information given five years later, at the Twenty-second Congress in 1961, startled and shocked the listeners anew. But we cannot blame Khrushchev for what was missing from his first statement. Before 1956, before the Congress, he could not yet prepare his speech officially and openly, he could not yet tell the whole truth; even so he had exposed himself to very great personal risk: Malenkov, Kaganovich, Voroshilov, Molotov, and Saburov, all people closely connected with the many acts of violence and repression committed by Stalin, were still strongly entrenched in the Presidium of the Central Committee and they would have undoubtedly done everything possible to remove Khrushchev from the leadership of the party, even before he had a chance to step on the podium on the night of 24 February 1956. In the summer of 1957 they were capable of preparing a plot against Khrushchev, but that plot proved abortive. Dismissed after three days of discussions in the Presidium, Khrushchev nevertheless managed to carry out a countercoup and, with the support of the majority of the Plenum and the leadership of the army and the KGB, to remove from the Central Committee the bulk of the members of the so-called "anti-party" group.

The unexpectedness of Khrushchev's speech created many problems which presently split the communist movement provoking bewilderment in many foreign parties, especially in the countries of the Soviet bloc which until then had only been imitating the policies of the Communist Party of the Soviet Union. The leaders of these countries had for a long time instituted the cult of their own personalities using terror and mass repressions to silence all dissent. Khrushchev had no choice — he could make his move either unexpectedly or he could not make it at all, continuing to conceal Stalin's misdeeds from the world, leaving to others, to bourgeois propagandists and historians the opportunity to "unmask" communism and socialism and to indentify the internal policy of socialist countries with oppression and arbitrariness.

The reasons for Khrushchev's decision to come forward with such determination at the Twentieth Congress were no doubt complex and contradictory. This was a considered political move, but there was also much in it that was impulsive and emotional. Placed at the head of the party after Stalin's death, Khrushchev had already in the first months to contend with the conspiracy of Beria who had been preparing to seize power in 1953. After Stalin died, Beria held in his hands the whole centralized machinery of repression: the Ministry of State Security combined with the Ministry of Interior. And this joint apparatus was already, in Stalin's time, autonomous: it was subject to the Party leadership neither at the centre nor in the provinces. Several divisions of the MVD [Ministry of the Interior], brought to Moscow to supervise Stalin's funeral, were left there on Beria's directive "to keep order". Beria was also responsible for the security of the Kremlin and all Governmental and Party establishments. At that same time Khrushchev was preparing a counter-action, supported by the majority of the members of the Presidium who, just like him, realized what was in store for them in the event that Beria and the so-called "Mafia of the Caucasus" around him were able to seize power. The decisive role in the liquidation of Beria and his group was played by the leadership of the army (Marshals Zhukov, Koniev and others). On the day of Beria's arrest, army detachments speedily detained all the security guards of the Kremlin and occupied government buildings in Moscow. The Central building of the MGB/MVD in Moscow was occupied by army units; many high officials who resisted arrest were shot in their own offices. Their bodies were later removed and buried in an unknown place.

All the establishments of state security in the Republics and in the provinces were dismantled, and, in a day or two the whole enormous machinery of repression had been liquidated. Only several months later the KGB came into existence, but this was an organization which was completely subordinate to the party leadership.

The investigation and inquiry into the activities of Beria and his closest associates revealed before the whole leadership of the Party the enormity of the crimes not only of Beria but also of Stalin, the details of which many party leaders had perceived only very dimly. The investigation inevitably set in motion the process of rehabilitation of many party leaders who had been imprisoned or murdered by Stalin, in the first instance of those imprisoned in the last years of Stalin's life, whose innocence was obvious to all. (N. Voznessensky, A. Voznessensky, the leadership of the Leningrad region, the leaders of the Council of Ministers of the RSFSR and many others imprisoned in 1949-1950 during the so-called "Leningrad affair"). A limited process of rehabilitation (in the majority of cases posthumously) affected also a number of the most prominent party members who perished in 1937-1938.

But this process was slow and at the time of the Twentieth Congress only a few thousand people, out of millions of innocents still languishing in prisons and camps, had been rehabilitated. The release of these people became possible only after February 1956. To speed up the process, on Khrushchev's directive over a hundred special commissions were set up, many headed by former inmates of the camps who had themselves been released between 1953 and 1955. These commissions, endowed with wide powers, left Moscow for the "islands" of the "Gulag Archipelago". Until the Twentieth Congress the cases of political prisoners could be reviewed only by the Supreme Court of the USSR or its Military Collegium. After the Congress the commissions despatched to camps were given the authority to revise these cases and to grant rehabilitation on the spot. Very often it was enough to become quickly acquainted with the documents of the case, to have a talk with the prisoner, and to learn about his political and party past, to rehabilitate him. Already by the summer of 1956 over five million political prisoners had been released from camps. Also released were those few Social Revolutionaries and Mensheviks imprisoned between 1928 and 1930 who had survived 26 or 28 years in camps and jails. Only by a miracle could one survive such long terms; even of those who were arrested and sentenced in 1936-1938 there remained alive in 1956 only 100,000: which is to say, only 5 per cent of those who had been engulfed by the cruellest terror. The bulk of the camp population in 1956 consisted of the victims of the war years and of the post-war repression.

The return of millions of ex-prisoners and the posthumous rehabilitation of many millions more, were the most weighty consequences of the Twentieth Congress for the internal life of the USSR. more important even than the revelations of Stalin's misdeeds. The direct indictment of Stalin in 1956 was not full enough and not consistent enough. In party histories he was still treated as a prominent leader and a classical Marxist, guilty only of some abuse of power and of having introduced the "cult of personality" of which many became the innocent victims. Dozens of cities still bore Stalin's name; his busts and monuments still decorated all towns and official buildings, his portraits still hung on the walls of party offices; his embalmed body was still on display next to Lenin's in the Mausoleum near the Kremlin. The final demolition of the Stalin "cult" took place in 1961 during the Twenty-second Congress, when — again unexpectedly — Khrushchev came forward with a new and long indictment, this time not at a "closed" meeting but at an open session of the Congress. Then Khrushchev also openly and clearly posed the problem of Stalin's accomplices.

This sharp turn in the proceedings of the Congress brought confusion into the ranks of the leaders; but it became impossible to avoid the examination of Stalin's crimes any longer. Main speakers set out quickly to re-write their speeches, so that they should include details of Stalin's detrimental acts towards the Party and the nation and also of the harmful activities of the "anti-party group". At the open sessions of the Congress crimes on a mass scale were revealed which by far surpassed all that had been learned from Khrushchev's own speeches of 1956 and 1961. This discredited Stalin and Stalinism finally and irrevocably. Before the end of the Congress on the night of 31 October 1961 Stalin's body was removed from the Mausoleum. Not far away from the Kremlin an excavator dug out a deep pit and into it Stalin's coffin was lowered. So that the body should not be dug up again, the pit was covered not with earth but with concrete. On top a granite slab was placed on which, only later, the name was engraved: "J.V. Stalin". A wave of destruction of Stalin's monuments swept over towns and villages; streets, kolkhozes, plants, settlements and cities were all renamed.

Khrushchev committed many mistakes and misjudgements during the time of his political leadership. Nor was he innocent of violations of the law in Stalin's time. He was not well equipped to run the economy and agriculture of the country competently; he was unable to create conditions for a genuine inner-party democracy, let alone a democratic way of life of the whole country. Yet all these mistakes and shortcomings of his leadership were only transitory. His main merit so far as the whole of mankind is concerned consists in the fact that he was able to overcome inertia and indecision, to mount the platform of the Twentieth Congress on the night of 24 February 1956 and to place before the whole communist movement the choice between a humanist and a totalitarian socialism. "Socialism with a human face" cannot come about too early; totalitarianism does not vanish after one speech: in changed forms it has continued for a long time. The ferment which Khrushchev engendered in 1956 still continues: it is a long historical process. And although Khrushchev's name is consigned to oblivion in the USSR and is unceasingly slandered in China and other communist countries, the process which began with his "secret" speech in 1956 cannot fail to bring nearer the advent of a humanist and open socialism, in which the rights of every individual will be defended, respected and firmly guaranteed.

N.S. Khrushchev's "secret speech", a special report to the closed session of the 20th Congress of the C.P.S.U., was delivered on the evening of 24-25 February, 1956, and subsequently published outside the Soviet Union on 4 June 1956, on the initiative of the U.S. State Department for Foreign Affairs.

Special Report
by N. S. Khrushchev to the Closed Session of the 20th Congress of the C.P.S.U.

2

Special Report

COMRADES! In the report of the Central Committee of the party at the 20th Congress, in a number of speeches by delegates to the Congress, as also formerly during the plenary CC/CPSU sessions, quite a lot has been said about the cult of the individual and about its harmful consequences.

After Stalin's death the Central Committee of the party began to implement a policy of explaining concisely and consistently that it is impermissible and foreign to the spirit of Marxism-Leninism to elevate one person, to transform him into a superman possessing supernatural characteristics, akin to those of a god. Such a man supposedly knows everything, sees everything, thinks for everyone, can do anything, is infallible in his behaviour.

Such a belief about a man, and specifically about Stalin, was cultivated among us for many years.

The objective of the present report is not a thorough evaluation of Stalin's life and activity. Concerning Stalin's merits, an entirely sufficient number of books, pamphlets and studies had already been written in his lifetime. The role of Stalin in the preparation and execution of the Socialist Revolution, in the Civil War, and in the fight for the construction of socialism in our country, is universally known. Everyone knows this well.

At present, we are concerned with a question which has immense importance for the party now and for the future — with how the cult of the person of Stalin has been gradually growing, the cult which became at a certain specific stage the source of a whole series of exceedingly serious and grave perversions of party principles, of party democracy, of revolutionary legality.

Because of the fact that not all as yet realize fully the practical consequences resulting from the cult of the individual, the great harm caused by the violation of the principle of collective direction of the party and because of the accumulation of immense and limitless power in the hands of one person, the Central Committee of the party considers it absolutely necessary to make the material pertaining to this matter available to the 20th Congress of the Communist Party of the Soviet Union.

Allow me first of all to remind you how severely the classics of Marxism-Leninism denounced every manifestation of the cult of the individual. In a letter to the German political worker, Wilhelm Bloss,[1] Marx stated:

"From my antipathy to any cult of the individual, I never made public during the existence of the International the numerous addresses from various countries which recognized my merits and which annoyed me. I did not even reply to them, except sometimes to rebuke their authors. Engels and I first joined the secret society of Communists on the condition that everything making for superstitious worship of authority would be deleted from its statute. Lassalle subsequently did quite the opposite."

Sometime later Engels wrote:

"Both Marx and I have always been against any public manifestation with regard to individuals, with the exception of cases when it had an important purpose; and we most strongly opposed such manifestations which during our lifetime concerned us personally."

The great modesty of the genius of the Revolution, Vladimir Ilyich Lenin, is known. Lenin had always stressed the role of the people as the creator of history, the directing and organizational role of the party as a living and creative organism, and also the role of the Central Committee.

Marxism does not negate the role of the leaders of the working class in directing the revolutionary liberation movement.

While ascribing great importance to the role of the leaders and organizers of the masses, Lenin at the same time mercilessly stigmatized every manifestation of the cult of the individual, inexorably combated the foreign-to-Marxism views about a "hero" and a "crowd", and countered all efforts to oppose a "hero" to the masses and to the people.

Lenin taught that the party's strength depends on its indissoluble unity with the masses, on the fact that behind the party follows the people — workers, peasants and intelligentsia. "Only he will win and retain power," said Lenin, "who believes in the people, who submerges himself in the fountain of the living creativeness of the people."

Lenin spoke with pride about the Bolshevik communist party as the leader and teacher of the people; he called for the presentation of all the most important questions before the opinion of knowledgeable workers, before the opinion of their party; he said' "We believe in it, we see in it the wisdom, the honour, and the conscience of our epoch."

Lenin resolutely stood against every attempt aimed at belittling or weakening the directing role of the party in the structure of the Soviet state. He worked out Bolshevik principles of party direction and norms of party life, stressing that the guiding principle of party leadership is its collegiality. Already during the pre-Revolutionary years, Lenin called the Central Committee of the party a collective of leaders and the guardian and interpreter of party principles. "During the period between congresses," pointed out Lenin, "the Central Committee guards and interprets the principles of the party."

Underlining the role of the Central Committee of the party and its authority, Vladimir Ilyich pointed out: "Our Central Committee constituted itself as a closely centralized and highly authoritative group."

During Lenin's life the Central Committee of the party was a real expression of collective leadership of the party and of the nation. Being a militant Marxist-revolutionist, always unyielding in matters of principle, Lenin never imposed by force his views upon his co-workers. He tried to convince; he patiently explained his opinions to others. Lenin always diligently observed that the norms of party life were realized, that the party statute was enforced, that the party congresses and the plenary sessions of the Central Committee took place at the proper intervals.

In addition to the great accomplishments of V.I. Lenin for the victory of the working class and of the working peasants, for the victory of our party and for the application of the ideas of scientific Communism to life, his acute mind expressed itself also in this — that he detected in Stalin in time those negative characteristics which resulted later in grave consequences. Fearing the future fate of the party and of the Soviet nation, V.I. Lenin made a completely correct characterization of Stalin, pointing out that it was necessary to consider the question of transferring Stalin from the position of the Secretary General because of the fact that Stalin is excessively rude, that he does not have a proper attitude towards his comrades, that he is capricious and abuses his power.

In December 1922, in a letter to the Party Congress, Vladimir Ilyich wrote:

"After taking over the position of Secretary General, Comrade Stalin accumulated in his hands immeasurable power and I am not certain whether he will be always able to use this power with the required care."

This letter — a political document of tremendous importance, known in the party history as Lenin's "testament" — was distributed among the delegates to the 20th Party Congress. You have read it and will undoubtedly read it again more than once. You might reflect on Lenin's plain words, in which expression is given to Vladimir Ilyich's anxiety concerning the party, the people, the state, and the future direction of party policy.

Vladimir Ilyich said:

"Stalin is excessively rude, and this defect, which can be freely tolerated in our midst and in contacts among us communists, becomes a defect which cannot be tolerated in one holding the position of the Secretary General. Because of this, I propose that the comrades consider the method by which Stalin would be removed from this position and by which another man would be selected for it, a man who, above all, would differ from Stalin in only one quality, namely, greater tolerance, greater loyalty, greater kindness and more considerate attitude toward the comrades, a less capricious temper, etc."

This document of Lenin's was made known to the delegates at the 13th Party Congress, who discussed the question of transferring Stalin from the position of Secretary General. The delegates declared themselves in favour of retaining Stalin in this post, hoping that he would heed the critical remarks of Vladimir Ilyich and would be able to overcome the defects which caused Lenin serious anxiety.

Comrades! The Party Congress should become acquainted with two new documents, which confirm Stalin's character as already outlined by Vladimir Ilyich Lenin in his "testament". These documents are a letter from Nadexhda Konstantinovna Krupskaya[2] to Kamenev,[3] who was at that time head of the Political Bureau, and a personal letter from Vladimir Ilyich Lenin to Stalin.

I will now read these documents:

"Lev Borisovich!
"Because of a short letter which I had written in words dictated to me by Vladimir Ilyich by permission of the doctors, Stalin allowed himself yesterday an unusually rude outburst directed at me. This is not my first day in the party. During all these 30 years I have never heard from any comrade one word of rudeness. The business of the party and of Ilyich are not less dear to me than to Stalin. I need at present the maximum of self-control. What one can and what one cannot discuss with Ilyich I know better than any doctor, because I know what makes him nervous and what does not, in any case I know better than Stalin. I am turning to you and to Grigory[4] as much closer comrades of V.I. and I beg you to protect me from rude interference with my private life and from vile invectives and threats. I have no doubt as to what will be the unanimous decision of the Control Commission with which Stalin sees fit to threaten me; however, I have neither the strength nor the time to waste on this foolish quarrel. And I am a living person and my nerves are strained to the utmost.

"N. Krupskaya"

Nadezhda Konstantinovna wrote this letter on December 23, 1922. After two and a half months, in March 1923, Vladimir Ilyich Lenin sent Stalin the following letter:

"To Comrade Stalin:
"Copies for Kamenev and Zinoviev.
"Dear Comrade Stalin!
"You permitted yourself, a rude summons of my wife to the telephone and a rude reprimand of her. Despite the fact that she told you that she agreed to forget what was said, nevertheless Zinoviev and Kamenev heard about it from her. I have no in-

tention to forget so easily that which is being done against me, and I need not stress here that I consider as directed against me that which is being done against my wife. I ask you, therefore, that you weigh carefully whether you are agreeable to retracting your words and apologizing or whether you prefer the severance of relations between us.
"March 5, 1923" "Sincerely: LENIN

(Commotion in the hall.)

Comrades! I will not comment on these documents. They speak eloquently for themselves. Since Stalin could behave in this manner during Lenin's life, could thus behave towards Nadezhda Konstantinovna Krupskaya — whom the party knows well and values highly as a loyal friend of Lenin and as an active fighter for the cause of the party since its creation — we can easily imagine how Stalin treated other people. These negative characteristics of his developed steadily and during the last years acquired an absolutely insufferable character.

As later events have proven, Lenin's anxiety was justified: in the first period after Lenin's death, Stalin still paid attention to his advice, but later he began to disregard the serious admonitions of Vladimir Ilyich.

When we analyze the practice of Stalin in regard to the direction of the party and of the country, when we pause to consider everything which Stalin perpetrated, we must be convinced that Lenin's fears were justified. The negative characteristics of Stalin, which, in Lenin's time, were only incipient, transformed themselves during the last years into a grave abuse of power by Stalin, which caused untold harm to our party.

We have to consider seriously and analyze correctly this matter in order that we may preclude any possibility of a repetition in any form whatever of what took place during the life of Stalin, who absolutely did not tolerate collegiality in leadership and in work, and who practiced brutal violence, not only toward everything which opposed him, but also toward that which seemed, to his capricious and despotic character, contrary to his concepts.

Stalin acted not through persuasion, explanation and patient cooperation with people, but by imposing his concepts and demanding absolute submission to his opinion. Whoever opposed this concept or tried to prove his viewpoint and the correctness of his position was doomed to removal from the leading collective and to subsequent moral and physical annihilation. This was especially true during the period following the 17th Party Congress,[5] when many prominent party leaders and rank-and-file party workers, honest and dedicated to the cause of Communism, fell victim to Stalin's despotism.

We must affirm that the party had fought a serious fight against the Trotskyites,[6] rightists and bourgeois nationalists, and that it disarmed ideologically all the enemies of Leninism. This ideological fight was carried on successfully, as a result of which the party became strengthened and tempered. Here Stalin played a positive role.

The party led a great political-ideological struggle against those in its own ranks who proposed anti-Leninist theses, who represented a political line hostile to the party and to the cause of socialism. This was a stubborn and a difficult fight but a necessary one, because the political line of both the Trotskyite-Zinovievite bloc and of the Bukharinites[7] led actually toward the restoration of capitalism and capitulation to the world bourgeoisie. Let us consider for a moment what would have happened if in 1928-1929 the political line of right deviation had prevailed among us, or orientation toward "cotton-dress industrialization," or toward the kulak, etc. We would not now have a powerful heavy industry, we would not have the kolkhozes, we would find ourselves disarmed and weak in a capitalist encirclement.

It was for this reason that the party led an inexorable ideological fight and explained to all party members and to the non-party masses the harm and the danger of the anti-Leninist proposals of the Trotskyite opposition and the rightist opportunists. And this great work of explaining the party line bore fruit; both the Trotskyites and the rightist opportunists were politically isolated; the overwhelming party majority supported the Leninist line and the party was able to awaken and organize the working masses to apply the Leninist Party line and to build socialism.

Worth noting is the fact that, even during the progress of the furious ideological fight against the Trotskyites, the Zinovievites, the Bukharinites and others, extreme repressive measures were not used against them. The fight was on ideological grounds. But some years later, when socialism in our country was fundamentally constructed, when the exploiting classes were generally liquidated, when the Soviet social structure had radically changed, when the social basis for political movements and groups hostile to the party had violently contracted, when the ideological opponents of the party were long since defeated politically — then the repression directed against them began.

It was precisely during this period (1935-1937-1938) that the practice of mass repression through the Government apparatus was born, first against the enemies of Leninism — Trotskyites, Zinovievites, Bukharinites, long since politically defeated by the party — and subsequently also against many honest Communists, against those party cadres who had borne the heavy load of the Civil War and the first and most difficult years of industrialization and collectivization, who actively fought against the Trotskyites and the rightists for the Leninist party line.

Stalin originated the concept "enemy of the people." This term automatically rendered it unnecessary that the ideological errors of a man or men engaged in a controversy be proven; this term made possible the usage of the most cruel repression, violating all norms of revolutionary legality, against anyone who in any way disagreed with Stalin, against those who were only suspected of hostile intent, against those who had bad reputations. This concept "enemy of the people" actually eliminated the possibility of any kind of ideological fight or the making of one's views known on this or that issue, even those of a practical character. In the main, and in actuality, the only proof of guilt used, against all norms of current legal science, was the "confession" of the accused himself; and, as subsequent probing proved, "confessions" were acquired through physical pressures against the accused. This led to glaring violations of revolutionary legality and to the fact that many entirely innocent persons, who in the past had defended the party line, became victims.

We must assert that, in regard to those persons who in their time had opposed the party line, there were often no sufficiently serious reasons for their physical annihilation. The formula "enemy of the people" was specifically introduced for the purpose of physically annihilating such individuals.

It is a fact that many persons who were later annihilated as enemies of the party and people had worked with Lenin during his life. Some of these persons had made errors during Lenin's life, but, despite this, Lenin benefited by their work; he corrected them and he did everything possible to retain them in the ranks of the party; he induced them to follow him.

In this connection the delegates to the Party Congress should familiarize themselves with an unpublished note by V.I. Lenin directed to the Central Committee's Political Bureau in October 1920. Outlining the duties of the Control Commission, Lenin wrote that the commission should be transformed into a real "organ of party and proletarian conscience."

"As a special duty of the Control Commission there is recommended a deep, individualized relationship with, and sometimes even a type of therapy for, the representatives of the so-called opposition — those who have experienced a psychological crisis because of failure in their Soviet or party career. An effort should be made to quiet them, to explain the matter to them in a way used among comrades, to find for them (avoiding the method of issuing orders) a task for which they are psychologically fitted. Advice and rules relating to this matter are to be formulated by the Central Committee's Organizational Bureau, etc."

Everyone knows how irreconcilable Lenin was with the ideological enemies of Marxism, with those who deviated from the correct party line. At the same time, however, Lenin, as is evident from the given document, in his practice of directing the party demanded the most intimate party contact with people who had shown indecision or temporary non-conformity with the party line, but whom it was possible to return to the party path. Lenin advised that such people should be patiently educated without the application of extreme methods.

Lenin's wisdom in dealing with people was evident in his work with cadres.

An entirely different relationship with people characterized Stalin. Lenin's traits — patient work with people, stubborn and painstaking education of them, the ability to induce people to follow him without using compulsion, but rather through the ideological influence on them of the whole collective — were entirely foreign to Stalin. He discarded the Leninist method of convincing and educating, he abandoned the method of ideological struggle for that of administrative violence, mass repressions and terror. He acted on an increasingly larger scale and more stubbornly through punitive organs, at the same time often violating all existing norms of morality and of Soviet laws.

Arbitrary behaviour by one person encouraged and permitted arbitrariness in others. Mass arrests and deportations of many thousands of people, execution without trial and without normal investigation created conditions of insecurity, fear and even desperation.

This, of course, did not contribute toward unity of the party ranks and of all strata of working people, but, on the contrary, brought about annihilation and the expulsion from the party of workers who were loyal but inconvenient to Stalin.

Our party fought for the implementation of Lenin's plans for the construction of socialism. This was an ideological fight. Had Leninist principles been observed during the course of this fight, had the party's devotion to principles been skilfully combined with a keen and solicitous concern for people, had they not been repelled and wasted but rather drawn to our side, we certainly would not have had such a brutal violation of revolutionary legality and many thousands of people would not have fallen victim to the method of terror. Extraordinary methods would then have been resorted to only against those people who had in fact committed criminal acts against the Soviet system.

Let us recall some historical facts.

In the days before the October Revolution, two members of the Central Committee of the Bolshevik Party — Kamenev and Zinoviev — declared themselves against Lenin's plan for an armed uprising. In addition, on October 18 they published in the Menshevik newspaper, *Novaya Zhizn,* a statement declaring that the Bolsheviks were making preparations for an uprising and that they considered it adventuristic. Kamenev and Zinoviev thus disclosed to the enemy the decision of the Central Committee to stage the uprising, and that the uprising had been organized to take place within the very near future.

This was treason against the party and against the Revolution. In this connection, V.I. Lenin wrote: "Kamenev and Zinoviev revealed the decision of the Central Committee of their party on the armed uprising to Rodzyanko[8] and Kerensky..." He put before the Central Committee the question of Zinoviev's and Kamenev's expulsion from the party.

However, after the Great Socialist October Revolution, as is known, Zinoviev and Kamenev were given leading positions. Lenin put them in positions in which they carried out most responsible party tasks and participated actively in the work of the leading party and Soviet organs. It is known that Zinoviev and Kamenev committed a number of other serious errors during Lenin's life. In his "testament" Lenin warned that "Zinoviev's and Kamenev's October episode was of course not an accident." But Lenin did not pose the question of their arrest and certainly not their shooting.

Or, let us take the example of the Trotskyites. At present, after a sufficiently long historical period, we can speak about the fight with the Trotskyites with complete calm and can analyze this matter with sufficient objectivity. After all, around Trotsky were people whose origin cannot by any means be traced to bourgeois society. Part of them belonged to the party intelligentsia and a certain part were recruited from among the workers. We can name many individuals who, in their time, joined the Trotskyites; however, these same individuals took an active part in the workers' movement before the Revolution, during the Socialist October Revolution itself, and also in the consolidation of the victory of this greatest of revolutions. Many of them broke with Trotskyism and returned to Leninist positions. Was it necessary to annihilate such people? We are deeply convinced that, had Lenin lived, such an extreme method would not have been used against any of them.

Such are only a few historical facts. But can it be said that Lenin did not decide to use even the most severe means against enemies of the Revolution when this was actually necessary? No; no one can say this. Vladimir Ilyich demanded uncompromising dealings with the enemies of the Revolution and of the working class and when necessary resorted ruthlessly to such methods. You will recall only V.I. Lenin's fight with the Social Revolutionary[9] organizers of the anti-Soviet uprising, with the counter-revolutionary kulaks in 1918 and with others, when Lenin without hesitation used the most extreme methods against the enemies. Lenin used such methods, however, only against actual class enemies and not against those who err, and whom it was possible to lead through ideological influence and even retain in the leadership. Lenin used severe methods only in the most necessary cases, when the exploiting classes were still in existence and were vigorously opposing the Revolution, when the struggle for survival was decidedly assuming the sharpest forms, even including a civil war.

Stalin, on the other hand, used extreme methods and mass repressions at a time when the Revolution was already victorious, when the Soviet state was strengthened, when the exploiting classes were already liquidated and socialist relations were rooted solidly in all phases of national economy, when our party was politically consolidated and had strengthened itself both numerically and ideologically.

It is clear that here Stalin showed in a whole series of cases his intolerance, his brutality and his abuse of power. Instead of proving his political correctness and mobilizing the masses, he often chose the path of repression and physical annihilation, not only against actual enemies, but also against individuals who had not committed any crimes against the party and the Soviet Government. Here we see no wisdom but only a demonstration of the brutal force which had once so alarmed V.I. Lenin.

Lately, especially after the unmasking of the Beria[10] gang, the Central Committee looked into a series of matters fabricated by this gang. This revealed a very ugly picture of brutal wilfulness connected with the incorrect behaviour of Stalin. As facts prove, Stalin, using his unlimited power, allowed himself many abuses, acting in the name of the Central Committee, not asking for the opinion of the Committee members nor even of the members of the Central Committee's Political Bureau; often he did not inform them about his personal decisions concerning very important party and governmental matters.

Considering the question of the cult of the individual, we must first of all show everyone what harm this caused to the interests of our party.

Vladimir Ilyich Lenin had always stressed the party's role and significance in the direction of the socialist government of workers and peasants; he saw in this the chief precondition for a successful building of socialism in our country. Pointing to the great responsibility of the Bolshevik party, as ruling party of the Soviet state, Lenin called for the most meticulous observance of all norms of party life; he called for the realization of the principles of collegiality in the direction of the party and the state.

Collegiality of leadership flows from the very nature of our party, a party built on the principles of democratic centralism.

"This means," said Lenin, "that all party matters are accomplished by all party members — directly or through representatives — who, without any exceptions, are subject to the same rules; in addition, all administrative members, all directing collegia, all holders of party positions are elective, they must account for their activities and are recallable."

It is known that Lenin himself offered an example of the most careful observance of these principles. There was no matter so important that Lenin himself decided it without asking for the advice and approval of the majority of the Central Committee members or of the members of the Central Committee's Political Bureau. In the most difficult period for our party and our country, Lenin considered it necessary regularly to convoke congresses, party conferences and plenary sessions of the Central Committee at which all the most important questions were discussed and where resolutions, carefully worked out by the collective of leaders, were approved.

We can recall, for an example, the year 1918 when the country was threatened by the attack of the imperialistic interventionists. In this situation the 7th Party Congress was convened in order to discuss a vitally important matter which could not be postponed — the matter of peace. In 1919, while the civil war was raging, the 8th Party Congress convened which adopted a new party programme, decided such important matters as the relationship with the peasant masses, the organization of the Red Army, the leading role of the party in the work of the soviets, the correction of the social composition of the party, and other matters. In 1920 the 9th Party Congress was convened which laid down guiding principles pertaining to the party's work in the sphere of economic construction. In 1921 the 10th Party Congress accepted Lenin's New Economic Policy[11] and the historical resolution called *About Party Unity*.

During Lenin's life, party congresses were convened regularly; always when a radical turn in the development of the party and the country took place, Lenin considered it absolutely necessary that the party discuss at length all the basic matters pertaining to internal and foreign policy and to questions bearing on the development of party and government.

It is very characteristic that Lenin addressed to the Party Congress as the highest party organ his last articles, letters and remarks.

During the period between congresses, the Central Committee of the party, acting as the most authoritative leading collective, meticulously observed the principles of the party and carried out its policy.

So it was during Lenin's life. Were our party's holy Leninist principles observed after the death of Vladimir Ilyich?

Whereas, during the first few years after Lenin's death, party congresses and Central Committee plenums took place more or less regularly, later, when Stalin began increasingly to abuse his power, these principles were brutally violated. This was especially evident during the last 15 years of his life. Was it a normal situation when over 13 years elapsed between the 18th and 19th Party Congresses,[12] years during which our party and our country had experienced so many important events? These events demanded categorically that the party should have passed resolutions pertaining to the country's defence during the Patriotic War and to peacetime construction after the war. Even after the end of the war a Congress was not convened for over seven years. Central Committee plenums were hardly ever called. It should be sufficient to mention that during all the years of the Patriotic War not a single Central Committee plenum took place. It is true that there was an attempt to call a Central Committee plenum in October 1941, when Central Committee members from the whole country were called to Moscow. They waited two days for the opening of the plenum, but in vain. Stalin did not even want to meet and talk to the Central Committee members. This fact shows how demoralized Stalin was in the first months of the war and how haughtily and disdainfully he treated the Central Committee members.

In practice, Stalin ignored the norms of party life and trampled on the Leninist principle of collective party leadership.

Stalin's wilfulness *vis-a-vis* the party and its Central Committee became fully evident after the 17th Party Congress which took place in 1934.

Having at its disposal numerous data showing brutal wilfulness toward party cadres, the Central Committee has created a party commission under the control of the Central Committee Presidium; it was charged with investigating what made possible mass repressions against the majority of the Central Committee members and candidates elected at the 17th Congress of the All-Union Communist Party (Bolsheviks).

The commission has become acquainted with a large quantity of materials in the NKVD archives and with other documents and has established many facts pertaining to the fabrication of cases against Communists, to false accusations, to glaring abuses of socialist legality, which resulted in the death of innocent people. It became apparent that many party, Soviet and economic activists, who were branded in 1937-1938 as "enemies", were actually never enemies, spies, wreckers, etc., but were always honest Communists; they were only so stigmatized and, often, no longer able to bear barbaric tortures, they charged themselves (at the order of the investigative judges — falsifiers) with all kinds of grave and unlikely crimes.

The commission has presented to the Central Committee Presidium lengthy and documented materials pertaining to mass repressions against the delegates to the 17th Party Congress and against members of the Central Committee elected at that Congress. These materials have been studied by the Presidium of the Central Committee.

It was determined that of the 139 members and candidates of the party's Central Committee who were elected at the 17th Congress, 98 persons, i.e. 70 per cent, were arrested and shot (mostly in 1937-1938). (Indignation in the hall.) What was the composition of the delegates to the 17th Congress? It is known that 80 per cent of the voting participants of the 17th Congress joined the party during the years of conspiracy before the Revolution and during the civil war; this means before 1921. By social origin the basic mass of the delegates to the Congress were workers (60 per cent of the voting members).

For this reason, it was inconceivable that a congress so composed would have elected a Central Committee a majority of whom would prove to be enemies of the party. The only reason why 70 per cent of the Central Committee members and candidates elected at the 17th Congress were branded as enemies of the party and of the people was because honest Communists were slandered, accusations against them were fabricated, and revolutionary legality was gravely undermined.

The same fate met not only the Central Committee members but also the majority of the delegates to the 17th Party Congress. Of 1,966 delegates with either voting or advisory rights, 1,108 persons were arrested on charges of anti-revolutionary crimes, i.e., decidedly more than a majority. This very fact shows how absurd, wild and contrary to common sense were the charges of counter-revolutionary crimes made out, as we now see, against a majority of participants at the 17th Party Congress. (Indignation in the hall.)

We should recall that the 17th Party Congress is historically known as the Congress of Victors. Delegates to the Congress were active participants in the building of our socialist state; many of them suffered and fought for party interests during the pre-Revolutionary years in the conspiracy and at the civil-war fronts; they fought their enemies valiantly and often nervelessly looked into the face of death.

How, then, can we believe that such people could prove to be "two-faced" and had joined the camps of the enemies of socialism during the era after the political liquidation of Zinovievites, Trotskyites and rightists and after the great accomplishments of socialist construction? This was the result of the abuse of power by Stalin, who began to use mass terror against the party cadres.

What is the reason that mass repressions against activists increased more and more after the 17th Party Congress? It was because at that time Stalin had so elevated himself above the party and above the nation that he ceased to consider either the Central Committee or the party.

While he still reckoned with the opinion of the collective before the 17th Congress, after the complete liquidation of the Trotskyites, Zinovievites and Bukharinites, when as a result of that fight and socialist victories the party achieved unity, Stalin ceased to an ever greater degree to consider the members of the party's Central Committee and even the members of the Political Bureau. Stalin thought that now he could decide all things alone and all he needed were statisticians; he treated all others in such a way that they could only listen to and praise him.

After the criminal murder of Sergei M. Kirov,[13] mass repressions and brutal acts of violation of socialist legality began. On the evening of December 1, 1934, on Stalin's initiative (without the approval of the Political Bureau — which was passed two days later, casually), the Secretary of the Presidium of the Central Executive Committee, Yenukidze,[14] signed the following directive:

"1. Investigative agencies are directed to speed up the cases of

those accused of the preparation or execution of acts of terror.
"2. Judicial organs are directed not to hold up the execution of death sentences, pertaining to crimes of this category in order to consider the possibility of pardon, because the Presidium of the Central Executive Committee of the USSR does not consider as possible the receiving of petitions of this sort.
"3. The organs of the Commissariat of Internal Affairs are directed to execute the death sentences against criminals of the above-mentioned category immediately after the passage of sentences."

This directive became the basis for mass acts of abuse against socialist legality. During many of the fabricated court cases, the accused were charged with "the preparation" of terroristic acts; this deprived them of any possibility that their cases might be re-examined, even when they stated before the court that their "confessions" were secured by force, and when, in a convincing manner, they disapproved the accusations against them.

It must be asserted that to this day the circumstances surrounding Kirov's murder hide many things which are inexplicable and mysterious and demand a most careful examination. There are reasons for the suspicion that the killer of Kirov, Nikolayev, was assisted by someone from among the people whose duty it was to protect the person of Kirov.

A month and a half before the killing, Nikolayev was arrested on the grounds of suspicious behaviour but he was released and not even searched. It is an unusually suspicious circumstance that when the Chekist assigned to protect Kirov was being brought for an interrogation, on December 2, 1934, he was killed in a car 'accident" in which no other occupants of the car were harmed. After the murder of Kirov, top functionaries of the Leningrad NKVD were given very light sentences, but in 1937 they were shot. We can assume that they were shot in order to cover the traces of the organizers of Kirov's killing. (Movement in the hall.)

Mass repressions grew tremendously from the end of 1936 after a telegram from Stalin and Zhdanov,[15] dated from Sochi on September 25, 1936, was addressed to Kaganovitch,[16] Molotov[17] and other members of the Political Bureau. The content of the telegram was as follows:

"We deem it absolutely necessary and urgent that Comrade

Yezhov[18] be nominated to the post of People's Commissar for Internal Affairs. Yagoda[19] has definitely proved himself to be incapable of unmasking the Trotskyite-Zinovievite bloc. The OGPU is four years behind in this matter. This is noted by all party workers and by the majority of the representatives of the KNVD."

Strictly speaking, we should stress that Stalin did not meet with and, therefore, could not know the opinion of party workers.

This Stalinist formulation that the "NKVD is four years behind" in applying mass repression and that there is a necessity for "catching up" with the neglected work directly pushed the NKVD workers on the path of mass arrests and executions.

We should state that this formulation was also forced on the February-March plenary session of the Central Committee of the All-Union Communist Party (Bolsheviks) in 1937. The plenary resolution approved it on the basis of Yezhov's report, *"Lessons Flowing from the Harmful Activity, Diversion and Espionage of the Japanese-German-Trotskyite Agents,"* stating:

"The plenum of the Central Committee of the All-Union Communist Party (Bolsheviks) considers that all facts revealed during the investigation into the matter of an anti-Soviet Trotskyite centre and of its followers in the provinces show that the People's Commissariat of Internal Affairs has fallen behind at least four years in the attempt to unmask these most inexorable enemies of the people."

The mass repressions at this time were made under the slogan of a fight against the Trotskyites. Did the Trotskyites at this time actually constitute such a danger to our party and to the Soviet state? We should recall that in 1927, on the eve of the 15th Party Congress, only some 4,000 votes were cast for the Trotskyite-Zinovievite opposition while there were 724,000 for the party line. During the 10 years which passed between the 15th Party Congress and the February-March Central Committee plenum, Trotskyism was completely disarmed; many former Trotskyites had changed their former views and worked in the various sectors building socialism. It is clear that in the situation of socialist victory there was no basis for mass terror in the country.

Stalin's report at the February-March Central Committee plenum in 1937, *"Deficiencies of Party Work and Methods for the Liquidation of the Trotskyites and of Other Two-Facers,"* contained an attempt at theoretical justification of the mass terror policy under the pretext that as we march forward toward socialism class war must allegedly sharpen. Stalin asserted that both history and Lenin taught him this.

Actually Lenin taught that the application of revolutionary violence is necessitated by the resistance of the exploiting classes, and this referred to the era when the exploiting classes existed and were powerful. As soon as the nation's political situation had improved, when in January 1920 the Red Army took Rostov and thus won a most important victory over Denikin,[20] Lenin instructed Dzerzshinsky[21] to stop mass terror and to abolish the death penalty. Lenin justified this important political move of the Soviet state in the following manner in his report at the session of the All-Union Central Executive Committee on February 2, 1920:

> "We were forced to use terror because of the terror practiced by the Entente, when strong world powers threw their hordes against us, not avoiding any type of conduct. We would not have lasted two days had we not answered these attempts of officers and White Guardists in a merciless fashion; this meant the use of terror, but this was forced upon us by the terrorist methods of the Entente.
>
> "But as soon as we attained a decisive victory, even before the end of the war, immediately after taking Rostov, we gave up the use of the death penalty and thus proved that we intend to execute our own programme in the manner that we promised. We say that the application of violence flows out of the decision to smother the exploiters, the big land-owners and the capitalists; as soon as this was accomplished we gave up the use of all extraordinary methods. We have proved this in practice."

Stalin deviated from these clear and plain precepts of Lenin. Stalin put the party and the NKVD up to the use of mass terror when the exploiting classes had been liquidated in our country and when there were no serious reasons for the use of extraordinary mass terror.

This terror was actually directed not at the remnants of the defeated exploiting classes but against the honest workers of the party and of the Soviet state; against them were made lying, slanderous and absurd accusations concerning "two-facedness," "espionage," "sabotage," preparation of fictitious "plots," etc.

At the February-March Central Committee plenum in 1937 many members actually questioned the rightness of the established course regarding mass repressions under the pretext of combating "two-facedness."

Comrade Postyshev[22] most ably expressed these doubts. He said:

"I have philosophized that the severe years of fighting have passed. Party members who have lost their backbones have broken down or have joined the camp of the enemy; healthy elements have fought for the party. These were the years of industrialization and collectivization. I never thought it possible that after this severe era had passed Karpov and people like him would find themselves in the camp of the enemy. (Karpov was a worker in the Ukrainian Central Committee whom Postyshev knew well.) And now, according to the testimony, it appears that Karpov was recruited in 1934 by the Trotskyites. I personally do not believe that in 1934 an honest party member who had trod the long road of unrelenting fight against enemies for the party and for socialism would now be in the camp of the enemies. I do not believe it . . . I cannot imagine how it would be possible to travel with the party during the difficult years and then, in 1934, join the Trotskyites. It is an odd thing . . ."

(Movement in the hall.)

Using Stalin's formulation, namely, that the closer we are to socialism the more enemies we will have, and using the resolution of the February-March Central Committee plenum passed on the basis of Yezhov's report, the *provocateurs* who had infiltrated the state-security organs together with conscienceless careerists began to protect with the party name the mass terror against party cadres, cadres of the Soviet state and the ordinary Soviet citizens. It should suffice to say that the number of arrests based on charges of counterrevolutionary crimes had grown ten times between 1936 and 1937.

It is known that brutal wilfulness was practiced against leading party workers. The party statute, approved at the 17th Party Congress, was based on Leninist principles expressed at the 10th Party

Congress. It stated that, in order to apply an extreme method such as exclusion from the party against a Central Committee member, against a Central Committee candidate and against a member of the Party Control Commission, "it is necessary to call a Central Committee plenum and to invite to the plenum all Central Committee candidate members and all members of the Party Control Commission"; only if two-thirds of the members of such a general assembly of responsible party leaders find it necessary, only then can a Central Committee member or candidate be expelled.

The majority of the Central Committee members and candidates elected at the 17th Congress and arrested in 1937-1938 were expelled from the party illegally through the brutal abuse of the party statute, because the question of their expulsion was never studied at the Central Committee plenum.

Now, when the cases of some of these so-called "spies" and "saboteurs" were examined, it was found that all their cases were fabricated. Confessions of guilt of many arrested and charged with enemy activity were gained with the help of cruel and inhuman tortures.

At the same time, Stalin, as we have been informed by members of the Political Bureau of that time, did not show them the statements of many accused political activists when they retracted their confessions before the military tribunal and asked for an objective examination of their cases. There were many such declarations, and Stalin doubtless knew of them.

The Central Committee considers it absolutely necessary to inform the Congress of many such fabricated "cases" against the members of the party's Central Committee elected at the 17th Party Congress.

An example of the vile provocation, of odious falsification and of criminal violation of revolutionary legality is the case of the former candidate for the Central Committee Political Bureau, one of the most eminent workers of the party and of the Soviet Government, Comrade Eikhe,[23] who was a party member since 1905. (Commotion in the hall.)

Comrade Eikhe was arrested on April 29, 1938, on the basis of slanderous materials, without the sanction of the Prosecutor of the USSR, which was finally received 15 months after the arrest.

Investigation of Eikhe's case was made in a manner which most brutally violated Soviet legality and was accompanied by wilfulness and falsification.

Eikhe was forced under torture to sign ahead of time a protocol of his confession prepared by the investigative judges, in which he and several other eminent party workers were accused of anti-Soviet activity.

On October 1, 1939, Eikhe sent his declaration to Stalin in which he categorically denied his guilt and asked for an examination of his case. In the declaration he wrote: "There is no more bitter misery than to sit in the jail of a government for which I have always fought."

A second declaration of Eikhe has been preserved which he sent to Stalin on October 27, 1939; in it he cited facts very convincingly and countered the slanderous accusations made against him, arguing that this provocatory accusation was on the one hand the work of real Trotskyites whose arrests he had sanctioned as First Secretary of the West Siberian Krai Party Committee and who conspired in order to take revenge on him, and, on the other hand, the result of the base falsification of materials by the investigative judges.

Eikhe wrote in his declaration:

" . . . On October 25 of this year I was informed that the investigation in my case has been concluded and I was given access to the materials of this investigation. Had I been guilty of only one hundredth of the crimes with which I am charged, I would not have dared to send you this pre-execution declaration; however, I have not been guilty of even one of the things with which I am charged and my heart is clean of even the shadow of baseness. I have never in my life told you a word of falsehood, and now, finding my two feet in the grave, I am also not lying. My whole case is a typical example of provocation, slander and violation of the elementary basis of revolutionary legality . . .

" . . . The confessions which were made part of my file are not only absurd but contain some slander towards the Central Committee of the All-Union Communist Party (Bolsheviks) and toward the Council of People's Commissars, because correct resoluttions of the Central Committee of the All-Union Communist Party (Bolsheviks) and of the Council of People's Commissars which were not made on my initiative and without my participation are presented as hostile acts of counter-revolutionary organizations made at my suggestion . . .

"I am now alluding to the most disgraceful part of my life and to my really grave guilt against the party and against you. This is my confession of counter-revolutionary activity . . . The case is as follows: Not being able to suffer the tortures to which I was submitted by Ushakov and Nikolayev — and especially by the first one — who utilized the knowledge that my broken ribs have not properly mended and have caused me great pain, I have been forced to accuse myself and others.

"The majority of my confession has been suggested or dictated by Ushakov, and the remainder is my reconstruction of NKVD materials from Western Siberia for which I assumed all responsibility. If some part of the story which Ushakov fabricated and which I signed did not properly hang together, I was forced to sign another variation. The same thing was done to Rukhimovich, who was at first designated as a member of the reserve net and whose name later was removed without telling me anything about it; the same was also done with the leader of the reserve net, supposedly created by Bukharin in 1935. At first I wrote my name in, and then I was instructed to insert Mezhlauk.[24] There were other similar incidents.

" . . . I am asking and begging you that you again examine my case, and this is not for the purpose of sparing me but in order to unmask the vile provocation which, like a snake, wound itself around many persons in a great degree due to my meanness and criminal slander. I have never betrayed you or the party. I know that I perish because of vile and mean work of the enemies of the party and of the people, who fabricated the provocation against me."

It would appear that such an important declaration was worth an examination by the Central Committee. This, however, was not done, and the declaration was transmitted to Beria while the terrible mal-treatment of the Political Bureau candidate, Comrade Eikhe, continued.

On February 2, 1940, Eikhe was brought before the court. Here he did not confess any guilt and said as follows:

"In all the so-called confessions of mine there is not one letter written by me with the exception of my signatures under the protocols, which were forced from me. I have made my confession under pressure from the investigative judge, who from the time of my arrest tormented me. After that I began to write all this nonsense . . . The most important thing for me is to tell the court, the party and Stalin that I am not guilty. I have never been guilty of any conspiracy. I will die believing in the truth of party policy as I have believed in it during my whole life."

On February 4 Eikhe was shot. (Indignation in the hall.)

It has been definitely established now that Eikhe's case was fabricated; he has been posthumously rehabilitated.

Comrade Rudzutak,[25] candidate-member of the Political Bureau, member of the party since 1905, who spent 10 years in a Tsarist hard-labour camp, completely retracted in court the confession which was forced from him. The protocol in the session of the Collegium of the Supreme Military Court contains the following statement by Rudzutak:

" . . . The only plea which he places before the court is that the Central Committee of the All-Union Communist Party (Bolsheviks) be informed that there is in the NKVD an as yet not liquidated centre which is craftily manufacturing cases, which forces innocent persons to confess; there is no opportunity to prove one's non-participation in crimes to which the confessions of various persons testify. The investigative methods are such that they force people to lie and to slander entirely innocent persons in addition to those who already stand accused. He asks the Court that he be allowed to inform the Central Committee of the All-Union Communist Party (Bolsheviks) about all this in writing. He assures the Court that he personally had never any evil designs in regard to the policy of our party because he had always agreed with the party policy pertaining to all spheres of economic and cultural activity."

This declaration of Rudzutak was ignored, despite the fact that Rudzutak was in his time the chief of the Central Control Commission, which was called into being in accordance with Lenin's concept for the purpose of fighting for party unity. In this manner fell the chief of this highly authoritative party organ, a victim of brutal wilfulness; he was not even called before the Central Committee's Political Bureau because Stalin did not want to talk to him. Sentence was pronounced on him in 20 minutes and he was shot. (Indignation in the hall.)

After careful examination of the case in 1955, it was established that the accusation against Rudzutak was false and that it was based on slanderous materials. Rudzutak has been rehabilitated posthumously.

The way in which the former NKVD workers manufactured various fictitious "anti-Soviet centres" and "blocs" with the help of provocatory methods is seen from the confession of Comrade Rozenblum, party member since 1906, who was arrested in 1937 by the Leningrad NKVD.

During the examination in 1955 of the Komarov case Rozenblum revealed the following fact: when Rozenblum was arrested in 1937, he was subjected to terrible torture during which he was ordered to confess false information concerning himself and other persons. He was then brought to the office of Zakovsky, who offered him freedom on condition that he make before the court a false confession fabricated in 1937 by the NKVD concerning "sabotage, espionage and diversion in a terroristic centre in Leningrad." (Movement in the hall.) With unbelievable cynicism, Zakovsky told about the vile "mechanism" for the crafty creation of fabricated "anti-Soviet plots."

Rozenblum stated:

"In order to illustrate it to me, Zakovsky gave me several possible variants of the organization of this centre and of its branches. After he detailed the organization to me, Zakovsky told me that the NKVD would prepare the case of this centre, remarking that the trial would be public. Before the court were to be brought 4 or 5 members of this centre: Chudov, Ugarov, Smorodin, Pozern, Shaposhnikova (Chudov's wife) and others together with 2 or 3 members from the branches of this centre . . .

" . . . The case of the Leningrad centre has to be built solidly, and for this reason witnesses are needed. Social origin (of course, in the past) and the party standing of the witness will play more than a small role.

" 'You, yourself,' said Zakovsky, 'will not need to invent anything. The NKVD will prepare for you a ready outline for every branch of the centre; you will have to study it carefully and to remember well all questions and answers which the Court might ask. This case will be ready in four-five months, or perhaps a half year. During all this time you will be preparing yourself so that you will not compromise the investigation and yourself.

Your future will depend on how the trial goes and on its results. If you begin to lie and to testify falsely, blame yourself. If you manage to endure it, you will save your head and we will feed and clothe you at the Government's cost until your death'."

This is the kind of vile things which were then practised. (Movement in the hall.)

Even more widely was the falsification of cases practised in the provinces. The NKVD headquarters of the Sverdlov Oblast "discovered" the so-called "Ural uprising staff" — an organ of the bloc of rightists, Trotskyites, Social Revolutionaries, church leaders — whose chief supposedly was the Secretary of the Sverdlov Oblast Party Committee and member of the Central Committee, All-Union Communist Party (Bolsheviks), Kabakov, who had been a party member since 1914. The investigative materials of that time show that in almost all krais, oblasts and republics there supposedly existed "rightist Trotskyite, espionage-terror and diversionary-sabotage organizations and centres" and that the heads of such organizations as a rule — for no known reason — were first secretaries of oblast or republic Communist party committees or central committees.

Many thousands of honest and innocent Communists have died as a result of this monstrous falsification of such "cases," as a result of the fact that all kinds of slanderous "confessions" were accepted, and as a result of the practice of forcing accusations against oneself and others. In the same manner were fabricated the "cases" against eminent party and state workers — Kossior,[26] Chubar,[27] Postyshev,[22] Kosarev[28] and others.

In those years repressions on a mass scale were applied which were based on nothing tangible and which resulted in heavy cadre losses to the party.

The vicious practice was condoned of having the NKVD prepare lists of persons whose cases were under the jurisdiction of the Military Collegium and whose sentences were prepared in advance. Yezhov would send these lists to Stalin personally for his approval of the proposed punishment. In 1937-1938, 383 such lists containing the names of many thousands of party, Soviet, Komsomol, Army and economic workers were sent to Stalin. He approved these lists.

A large part of these cases are being reviewed now and a great part of them are being voided because they were baseless and falsified. Suffice it to say that from 1954 to the present time the Military Collegium of the Supreme Court has rehabilitated 7,679 persons, many of whom were rehabilitated posthumously.

Mass arrests of party, Soviet, economic and military workers caused tremendous harm to our country and to the cause of socialist advancement.

Mass repressions had a negative influence on the moral-political condition of the party, created a situation of uncertainty, contributed to the spreading of unhealthy suspicion, and sowed distrust among Communists. All sorts of slanders and careerists were active.

Resolutions of the January plenum of the Central Committee, All-Union Communist Party (Bolsheviks), in 1938 had brought some measure of improvement to the party organizations. However, widespread repression also existed in 1938.

Only because our party has at its disposal such great moral political strength was it possible for it to survive the difficult events in 1937-1938 and to educate new cadres. There is, however, no doubt that our march forward toward socialism and toward the preparation of the country's defence would have been much more successful were it not for the tremendous loss in the cadres suffered as a result of the baseless and false mass repressions in 1937-38.

We are justly accusing Yezhov for the degenerate practices of 1937. But we have to answer these questions:

Could Yezhov have arrested Kossior, for instance, without the knowledge of Stalin? Was there an exchange of opinions or a Political Bureau decision concerning this?

No, there was not, as there was none regarding other cases of this type.

Could Yezhov have decided such important matters as the fate of such eminent party figures?

No, it would be a display of naivete to consider this the work of Yezhov alone. It is clear that these matters were decided by Stalin, and that without his orders and his sanction Yezhov could not have done this.

We have examined the cases and have rehabilitated Kossior, Rudzutak, Postyshev, Kosarev and others. For what causes were they arrested and sentenced? The review of evidence shows that there was no reason for this. They, like many others, were arrested without the prosecutor's knowledge.

In such a situation, there is no need for any sanction, for what sort of a sanction could there be when Stalin decided everything? He was the chief prosecutor in these cases. Stalin not only agreed to, but on his own initiative issued, arrest orders. We must say this so that the delegates to the Congress can clearly undertake and themselves assess this and draw the proper conclusions.

Facts prove that many abuses were made on Stalin's orders without reckoning with any norms of party and Soviet legality. Stalin was a very distrustful man, sickly suspicious; we know this from our work with him. He could look at a man and say: "Why are your eyes so shifty today?" or "Why are you turning so much today and avoiding to look me directly in the eyes?" The sickly suspicion created in him a general distrust even toward eminent party workers whom he had known for years. Everywhere and in everything he saw "enemies," "two-facers" and "spies". Possessing unlimited power, he indulged in great wilfulness and choked a person morally and physically. A situation was created where one could not express one's own will.

When Stalin said that one or another should be arrested, it was necessary to accept on faith that he was an "enemy of the people." Meanwhile, Beria's gang, which ran the organs of state security, outdid itself in proving the guilt of the arrested and the truth of materials which it falsified. And what proofs were offered? The confessions of the arrested, and the investigative judges accepted these "confessions." And how is it possible that a person confesses to crimes which he has not committed? Only in one way — because of application of physical methods of pressuring him, tortures, bringing him to a state of unconsciousness, deprivation of his judgement, taking away of his human dignity. In this manner were "confessions" acquired.

When the wave of mass arrests began to recede in 1939, and the leaders of territorial party organizations began to accuse the NKVD workers of using methods of physical pressure on the arrested, Stalin dispatched a coded telegram on January 20, 1939, to the committee secretaries of oblasts and krais, to the central committees of republic Communist parties, to the People's Commissars of Internal Affairs and to the heads of the NKVD organizations. This telegram stated:

"The Central Committee of the All-Union Communist Party (Bolsheviks) explains that the application of methods of physical pressure in NKVD practice is permissible from 1937 on in accordance with permission of the Central Committee of the All-Union Communist Party (Bolsheviks) . . . It is known that all bourgeois intelligence services use methods of physical influence against the representatives of the socialist proletariat and that they use them in their most scandalous forms.

"The question arises as to why the socialist intelligence service should be more humanitarian against the mad agents of the bourgeoisie, against the deadly enemies of the working class and of the kolkhoz workers. The Central Committee of the All-Union Communist Party (Bolsheviks) considers that physical pressure should still be used obligatorily, as an exception applicable to known and obstinate enemies of the people, as a method both justifiable and appropriate."

Thus, Stalin had sanctioned in the name of the Central Committee of the All-Union Communist Party (Bolsheviks) the most brutal violation of socialist legality, torture and oppression, which led as we have seen to the slandering and self-accusation of innocent people.

Not long ago — only several days before the present Congress — we called to the Central Committee Presidium session and interrogated the investigative judge Rodos, who in his time investigated and interrogated Kossior, Chubar and Kosarev. He is a vile person, with the brain of a bird, and morally completely degenerate. And it was this man who was deciding the fate of prominent party workers; he was making judgments also concerning the politics in these matters, because, having established their "crime," he provided therewith materials from which important political implications could be drawn.

The question arises whether a man with such an intellect could alone make the investigation in a manner to prove the guilt of people such as Kossior and others. No, he could not have done it without proper directives. At the Central Committee Presidium session he told us:

"I was told that Kossior and Chubar were people's enemies and for this reason I, as an investigative judge, had to make them confess that they are enemies." (Indignation in the hall.)

He would do this only through long tortures, which he did, receiving detailed instructions from Beria. We must say that at the Central Committee Presidium session he cynically declared: "I thought that I was executing the orders of the party." In this manner, Stalin's orders concerning the use of methods of physical pressure against the arrested were in practice executed.

These and many other facts show that all norms of correct party solution of problems were invalidated and everything was dependent upon the wilfulness of one man.

The power accumulated in the hands of one person, Stalin, led to serious consequences during the Great Patriotic War.

When we look at many of our novels, films and historical "scientific studies," the role of Stalin in the Patriotic War appears to be entirely improbable. Stalin had foreseen everything. The Soviet Army, on the basis of a strategic plan prepared by Stalin long before, used the tactics of so-called "active defence," i.e., tactics which, as we know, allowed the Germans to come up to Moscow and Stalingrad. Using such tactics, the Soviet Army, supposedly thanks to Stalin's genius, turned to the offensive and subdued the enemy. The epic victory gained through the armed might of the land of the Soviets, through our heroic people, is ascribed in this type of novel, firm and "scientific study" as being completely due to the strategic genius of Stalin.

We have to analyze this matter carefully because it has a tremendous significance not only from the historical, but especially from the political, educational and practical point of view. What are the facts of this matter?

Before the war, our press and all our political-educational work was characterized by its bragging tone: when an enemy violates the holy Soviet soil, then for every blow of the enemy we will answer with three blows, and we will battle the enemy on his soil and we will win without much harm to ourselves. But these positive statements were not based in all areas on concrete facts, which would actually guarantee the immunity of our borders.

During the war and after the war, Stalin put forward the thesis that the tragedy which our nation experienced in the first part of the war was the result of the "unexpected" attack of the Germans against the Soviet Union. But, comrades, this is completely untrue. As soon as Hitler came to power in Germany he assigned to himself the task of liquidating Communism. The fascists were saying this openly: they did not hide their plans.

In order to attain this aggressive end, all sorts of pacts and blocs were created, such as the famous Berlin-Rome-Tokyo Axis. Many facts from the pre-war period clearly showed that Hitler was going all out to begin a war against the Soviet state, and that he had concentrated large armed units, together with armoured units, near the Soviet borders.

Documents which have now been published show that by April 3, 1941, Churchill, through his Ambassador to the USSR, Cripps, personally warned Stalin that the Germans had begun regrouping their armed units with the intent of attacking the Soviet Union.

It is self-evident that Churchill did not do this at all because of his friendly feeling toward the Soviet nation. He had in this his own imperialistic goals — to bring Germany and the USSR into a bloody war and thereby to strengthen the position of the British Empire.

Just the same, Churchill affirmed in his writings that he sought to "warn Stalin and call his attention to the danger which threatened him." Churchill stresses this repeatedly in his dispatches of April 18 and on the following days. However, Stalin took no heed of these warnings. What is more, Stalin ordered that no credence be given to information of this sort, in order not to provoke the initiation of military operations.

We must assert that information of this sort concerning the threat of German armed invasion of Soviet territory was coming in also from our own military and diplomatic sources; however, because the leadership was conditioned against such information, such data was dispatched with fear and assessed with reservation.

Thus, for instance, information sent from Berlin on May 6, 1941, by the Soviet military attache, Captain Vorontsov, stated:

> "Soviet citizen Bozer . . . communicated to the deputy naval attache that, according to a statement of a certain German officer from Hitler's headquarters, Germany is preparing to invade the USSR on May 14 through Finland, the Baltic countries and Latvia. At the same time Moscow and Leningrad will be heavily raided and paratroopers landed in border cities . . .'"

In his report of May 22, 1941, the deputy military attache in Berlin, Khlopov, communicated that:

" . . . the attack of the German Army is reportedly scheduled for June 15, but it is possible that it may begin in the first days of June . . ."

A cable from our London Embassy dated June 18, 1941, stated:

"As of now Cripps is deeply convinced of the inevitability of armed conflict between Germany and the USSR, which will begin not later than the middle of June. According to Cripps, the Germans have presently concentrated 147 divisions (including air force and service units) along the Soviet borders . . ."

Despite these particularly grave warnings, the necessary steps were not taken to prepare the country properly for defence and to prevent it from being caught unawares.

Did we have time and the capabilities for such preparations? Yes, we had the time and capabilities. Our industry was already so developed that it was capable of supplying fully the Soviet Army with everything that it needed. This is proven by the fact that, although during the war we lost almost half of our industry and important industrial and food-production areas as the result of enemy occupation of the Ukraine, Northern Caucasus and other western parts of the country, the Soviet nation was still able to organize the production of military equipment in the eastern parts of the country, install there equipment taken from the western industrial areas, and to supply our armed forces with everything which was necessary to destroy the enemy.

Had our industry been mobilized properly and in time to supply the Army with the necessary material, our wartime losses would have been decidedly smaller. Such mobilization had not been, however, started in time. And already in the first days of the war it became evident that our Army was badly armed, that we did not have enough artillery, tanks and planes to throw the enemy back.

Soviet science and technology produced excellent models of tanks and artillery pieces before the war. But mass production of all this was not organized, and, as a matter of fact, we started to modernize our military equipment only on the eve of the war. As a result, at the time of the enemy's invasion of the Soviet land we did not have sufficient quantities either of old machinery which was no longer used for armament production or of new machinery which we had planned to introduce into armament production.

The situation with anti-aircraft artillery was especially bad; we did not organize the production of anti-tank ammunition. Many fortified regions had proven to be indefensible as soon as they were attacked, because the old arms had been withdrawn and new ones were not yet available there.

This pertained, alas, not only to tanks, artillery and planes. At the outbreak of the war we did not have sufficient numbers of rifles to arm the mobilized manpower. I recall that in those days I telephoned to Comrade Malenkov from Kiev and told him, "People have volunteered for the new Army and demand arms. You must send us arms."

Malenkov answered me,

> "We cannot send you arms. We are sending all our rifles to Leningrad and you have to arm yourselves." (Movement in the hall.)

Such was the armament situation.

In this connection we cannot forget, for instance, the following fact: shortly before the invasion of the Soviet Union by the Hitlerite army, Kirponos, who was chief of the Kiev Special Military District (he was later killed at the front), wrote to Stalin that the German armies were at the Bug River, were preparing for an attack and in the very near future would probably start their offensive. In this connection, Kirponos proposed that a strong defence be organized, that 300,000 people be evacuated from the border areas and that several strong points be organized there: anti-tank ditches, trenches for the soldiers, etc.

Moscow answered this proposition with the assertion that this would be a provocation, that no preparatory defensive work should be undertaken at the borders, that the Germans were not to be given any pretext for the initiation of military action against us. Thus, our borders were insufficiently prepared to repel the enemy.

When the fascist armies had actually invaded Soviet territory and military operations began, Moscow issued the order that the German fire was not to be returned. Why? It was because Stalin, despite evident facts, thought that the war had not yet started, that this was only a provocative action on the part of several undisciplined sections of the German Army, and that reaction might serve as a reason for the Germans to begin the war.

The following fact is also known: on the eve of the invasion of the territory of the Soviet Union by the Hitlerite army, a certain German citizen crossed our border and stated that the German armies had received orders to start the offensive against the Soviet Union on the night of June 22 at 3 o'clock. Stalin was informed about this immediately, but even this warning was ignored.

As you see, everything was ignored: warnings of certain Army commanders, declarations of deserters from the enemy army, and even the open hostility of the enemy. Is this an example of the alertness of the chief of the party and of the state at this particularly significant historical moment?

And what were the results of this carefree attitude, this disregard of clear facts? The result was that already in the first hours and days the enemy had destroyed in our border regions a large part of our Air Force, artillery and other military equipment; he annihilated large numbers of our military cadres and disorganized our military leadership; consequently we could not prevent the enemy from marching deep into the country.

Very grievous consequences, especially in reference to the beginning of the war, followed Stalin's annihilation of many military commanders and political workers during 1937-1941 because of his suspiciousness and through slanderous accusations. During these years repressions were instituted against certain parts of military cadres beginning literally at the company and battalion commander level and extending to the higher military centres; during this time the cadre of leaders who had gained military experience in Spain and in the Far East was almost completely liquidated.

The policy of large-scale repression against the military cadres led also to undermined military discipline, because for several years officers of all ranks and even soldiers in the party and Komsomol cells were taught to "unmask" their superiors as hidden enemies. (Movement in the hall.) It is natural that this caused a negative influence on the state of military discipline in the first war period.

And, as you know, we had before the war excellent military cadres which were unquestionably loyal to the party and to the Fatherland. Suffice it to say that those of them who managed to survive, despite severe tortures to which they were subjected in the prisons, have from the first war days shown themselves real patriots and heroically fought for the glory of the Fatherland; I have here in mind such comrades as Rokossovsky (who, as you know, had been jailed), Gorbatov, Maretskov (who is a delegate at the present Congress), Podlas (he was an excellent commander who perished at the front), and many many others. However, many such commanders perished in camps and jails and the Army saw them no more.

All this brought about the situation which existed at the beginning of the war and which was the great threat to our Fatherland.

It would be incorrect to forget that, after the first severe disaster and defeat at the front, Stalin thought that this was the end. In one of his speeches in those days he said: "All that which Lenin created we have lost forever."

After this Stalin for a long time actually did not direct the military operations and ceased to do anything whatever. He returned to active leadership only when some members of the Political Bureau visited him and told him that it was necessary to take certain steps immediately in order to improve the situation at the front.

Therefore, the threatening danger which hung over our Fatherland in the first period of the war was largely due to the faulty methods of directing the nation and the party by Stalin himself.

However, we speak not only about the moment when the war began, which led to serious disorganization of our Army and brought us severe losses. Even after the war began, the nervousness and hysteria which Stalin demonstrated, interfering with actual military operation, caused our Army serious damage.

Stalin was very far from an understanding of the real situation which was developing at the front. This was natural because, during the whole Patriotic War, he never visited any section of the front or any liberated city except for one short ride on the Mozhaisk highway during a stabilized situation at the front. To this incident were dedicated many literary works full of fantasies of all sorts and so many paintings. Simultaneously, Stalin was interfering with operations and issuing orders which did not take into consideration the real situation at a given section of the front and which could not help but result in huge personnel losses.

I will allow myself in this connection to bring out one characteristic fact which illustrates how Stalin directed operations at the fronts. There is present at this Congress Marshal Bagramian, who was once the chief of operations in the headquarters of the southwestern front and who can corroborate what I will tell you.

When there developed an exceptionally serious situation for our Army in 1942 in the Kharkov region, we had correctly decided to drop an operation whose objective was to encircle Kharkov, because the real situation at that time would have threatened our Army with fatal consequences if this operation was continued.

We communicated this to Stalin, stating that the situation demanded changes in operational plans so that the enemy would be prevented from liquidating a sizable concentration of our Army.

Contrary to common sense, Stalin rejected our suggestion and issued the order to continue the operation aimed at the encirclement of Kharkov, despite the fact that at this time many Army concentrations were themselves actually threatened with encirclement and liquidation.

I telephoned to Vasilevsky and begged him: "Alexander Mikhailovich, take a map" — Vasilevsky is present here — "and show Comrade Stalin the situation which has developed." We should note that Stalin planned operations on a globe. (Animation in the hall.) Yes, comrades, he used to take the globe and trace the front line on it. I said to Comrade Vasilevsky: "Show him the situation on a map; in the present situation we cannot continue the operation which was planned. The old decision must be changed for the good of the cause."

Vasilevsky replied, saying that Stalin had already studied this problem and that he, Vasilevsky, would not see Stalin further concerning this matter, because the latter didn't want to hear any arguments on the subject of this operation.

After my talk with Vasilevsky, I telephoned to Stalin in his villa. But Stalin did not answer the telephone and Malenkov was at the receiver. I told Comrade Malenkov that I was calling from the front and that I wanted to speak personally to Stalin. Stalin informed me through Malenkov that I should speak with Malenkov. I stated for the second time that I wished to inform Stalin personally about the grave situation which had arisen for us at the front. But Stalin did not consider it convenient to raise the phone and again stated that I should speak to him through Malenkov, although he was only a few steps from the telephone.

After "listening" in this manner to our plea, Stalin said: "Let everything remain as it is!"

And what was the result of this? The worst that we had expected. The Germans surrounded our Army concentrations and consequently we lost hundreds of thousands of our soldiers. This is Stalin's military "genius"; this is what it cost us. (Movement in the hall.)

On one occasion after the war, during a meeting of Stalin with members of the Political Bureau, Anastas Ivanovich Mikoyan mentioned that Khrushchev must have been right when he telephoned concerning the Kharkov operation and that it was unfortunate that his suggestion had not been accepted.

You should have seen Stalin's fury! How could it be admitted that he, Stalin, had not been right! He is after all a "genius," and a genius cannot help but be right! Everyone can err, but Stalin considered that he never erred, that he was always right. He never acknowledged to anyone that he made any mistake, large or small, despite the fact that he made not a few mistakes in the matter of theory and in his practical activity. After the Party Congress we shall probably have to re-evaluate many wartime military operations and to present them in their true light.

The tactics on which Stalin insisted without knowing the essence of the conduct of battle operations cost us much blood until we succeeded in stopping the opponent and going over to the offensive.

The military know that already by the end of 1941, instead of great operational maneouvres flanking the opponent and penetrating behind his back, Stalin demanded incessant frontal attacks and the capture of one village after another.

Because of this, we paid with great losses — until our generals, on whose shoulders rested the whole weight of conducting the war, succeeded in changing the situation and shifting to flexible-manoeuvre operations, which immediately brought serious changes at the front favourable to us.

All the more shameful was the fact that, after our great victory over the enemy whic cost us so much, Stalin began to downgrade many of the commanders who contributed so much to the victory over the enemy, because Stalin excluded every possibility that services rendered at the front should be credited to anyone but himself.

Stalin was very much interested in the assessment of Comrade Zhukov as a military leader. He asked me often for my opinion of Zhukov. I told him them, "I have known Zhukov for a long time; he is a good general and a good military leader."

After the war Stalin began to tell all kinds of nonsense about Zhukov, among others the following, "You praised Zhukov, but he does not deserve it. It is said that before each operation at the front Zhukov used to behave as follows: he used to take a handful of earth, smell it and say, 'We can begin the attack,' or the opposite. 'The planned operation cannot be carried out'." I stated at that time, "Comrade Stalin, I do not know who invented this, but it is not true."

It is possible that Stalin himself invented these things for the purpose of minimizing the role and military talents of Marshal Zhukov.

In this connection, Stalin very energetically popularized himself as a great leader; in various ways he tried to inculcate in the people the version that all victories gained by the Soviet nation during the Great Patriotic War were due to the courage, daring and genius of Stalin and of no one else. Exactly like Kuzma Kryuchkov[29] he put one dress on seven people at the same time. (Animation in the hall.)

In the same vein, let us take, for instance, our historical and military films and some literary creations; they make us feel sick. Their true objective is the propagation of the theme of praising Stalin as a military genius. Let us recall the film, *The Fall of Berlin*. Here only Stalin acts; he issues orders in the hall in which there are many empty chairs and only one man approached him and reports something to him — that is Poskrebyshev,[30] his loyal shield-bearer. (Laughter in the hall.)

And where is the military command? Where is the Political Bureau? Where is the Government? What are they doing and with what are they engaged? There is nothing about them in the film. Stalin acts for everybody; he does not reckon with anyone; he asks no one for advice. Everything is shown to the nation in this false light. Why? In order to surround Stalin with glory, contrary to the facts and contrary to historical truth.

The question arises: and where are the military, on whose shoulders rested the burden of the war? They are not in the film; with Stalin in, no room was left for them.

Not Stalin, but the party as a whole, the Soviet Government, our heroic Army, its talented leaders and brave soldiers, the whole Soviet nation — these are the ones who assured the victory of the Great Patriotic War. (Tempestuous and prolonged applause.)

The Central Committee members, ministers, our economic leaders, leaders of Soviet culture, directors of territorial-party and Soviet organizations, engineers, and technicians — every one of them in his own place of work generously gave of his strength and knowledge toward ensuring victory over the enemy.

Exceptional heroism was shown by our hard core — surrounded by glory is our whole working class, our kolkhoz peasantry, the Soviet intelligentsia, who under the leadership of party organizations over-came untold hardships and, bearing the hardships of war, devoted all their strength to the cause of the defence of the Fatherland.

Great and brave deeds during the war were accomplished by our Soviet women who bore on their backs the heavy load of production work in the factories, on the kolkhozes, and in various economic and cultural sectors; many women participated directly in the Great Patriotic War at the fronts; our brave youth contributed immeasurably at home to the defence of the Soviet Fatherland and to the annihilation of the enemy.

Immortal are the services of the Soviet soldiers, of our commanders and political workers of all ranks; after the loss of a considerable part of the Army in the first war months they did not lose their heads and were able to reorganize during the progress of combat; they created and toughened during the progress of the war a strong and heroic Army and not only stood off pressures of the strong and cunning enemy but also smashed him.

The magnificent and heroic deeds of hundreds of millions of people of the East and of the West during the fight against the threat of fascist subjugation which loomed before us will live centuries and millennia in the memory of thankful humanity. (Thunderous applause.)

The main role and the main credit for the victorious ending of the war belong to our Communist party, to the armed forces of the Soviet Union, and to the tens of millions of Soviet people raised by the party. (Thunderous and prolonged applause.)

Comrades, let us reach for some others facts. The Soviet Union is justly considered as a model of a multinational state because we have in practice assured the equality and friendship of all nations which live in our great Fatherland.

All the more monstrous are the acts whose initiator was Stalin and which are rude violations of the basic Leninist principles of the nationality policy of the Soviet state. We refer to the mass deportations from their native places of whole nations, together with all Communists and Komsomols without any exception; this deportation action was not dictated by any military considerations.

Thus, already at the end of 1943, when there occurred a permanent break-through at the fronts of the Great Patriotic War benefiting the Soviet Union, a decision was taken and executed concerning the deportation of all the Karachai from the lands on which they lived.

In the same period, at the end of December 1943, the same lot befell the whole population of the Autonomous Kalmyk Republic. In March 1944, all the Chechen and Ingush peoples were deported and the Chechen-Ingush Autonomous Republic was liquidated. In April 1944, all Balkars were deported to faraway places from the territory of the Kabardino-Balkar Autonomous Republic and the Republic itself was renamed the Autonomous Kabardian Republic.

The Ukrainians avoided meeting this fate only because there were too many of them and there was no place to which to deport them. Otherwise, he would have deported them also. (Laughter and animation in the hall.)

Not only a Marxist-Leninist but also no man of common sense can grasp how it is possible to make whole nations responsible for inimical activity, including women, children, old people, Communists and Komsomols, to use mass repression against them, and to expose them to misery and suffering for the hostile acts of individual persons or groups of persons.

After the conclusion of the Patriotic War, the Soviet nation stressed with pride the magnificent victories gained through great sacrifices and tremendous efforts. The country experienced a period of political enthusiasm. The party came out of the war even more united; in the fire of the war, party cadres were tempered and hardened. Under such conditions nobody could have even thought of the possibility of some plot in the party.

And it was precisely at this time that the so-called "Leningrad affair"[31] was born. As we have now proven, this case was fabricated. Those who innocently lost their lives and includes Comrades Voznessensky, Kuznetsov, Rodionov, Popkov, and others.

As is known, Voznessensky and Kuznetsov were talented and eminent leaders. Once they stood very close to Stalin. It is sufficient to mention that Stalin made Voznessensky first deputy to the chairman of the Council of Ministers and Kuznetsov was elected secretary of the Central Committee. The very fact that Stalin entrusted Kuznetsov with the supervision of the state security organs shows the trust which he enjoyed.

How did it happen that these persons were branded as enemies of the people and liquidated?

Facts prove that the "Leningrad affair" is also the result of wilfulness which Stalin exercised against party cadres. Had a normal situation existed in the party's Central Committee and in the Central Committee Political Bureau, affairs of this nature would have been examined there in accordance with party practice, and all pertinent facts assessed; as a result, such an affair as well as others would not have happened.

We must state that, after the war, the situation became even more complicated. Stalin became even more capricious, irritable and brutal; in particular his suspicion grew. His persecution mania reached unbelievable dimensions. Many workers were becoming enemies before his very eyes. After the war, Stalin separated himself from the collective even more. Everything was decided by him alone without any consideration for anyone or anything.

This unbelievable suspicion was cleverly taken advantage of by the abject *provocateur* and vile enemy, Beria, who had murdered thousands of Communists and loyal Soviet people. The elevation of Voznesensky and Kuznetsov alarmed Beria. As we have now proven, it had been precisely Beria who had "suggested" to Stalin the fabrication by him and by his confidants of materials in the form of declarations and anonymous letters, and in the form of various rumours and talks.

The party's Central Committee has examined this so-called "Leningrad affair"; persons who innocently suffered are now rehabilitated and honour has been restored to the glorious Leningrad party organization. Abakumov[32] and others who had fabricated this affair were brought before a court; their trial took place in Leningrad and they received what they deserved.

The question arises: why is it that we see the truth of this affair only now, and why did we not do something earlier, during Stalin's life, in order to prevent the loss of innocent lives? It was because Stalin personally supervised the "Leningrad affair", and the majority of the Political Bureau members did not, at that time, know all of the circumstances in these matters and could not therefore intervene.

When Stalin received certain material from Beria and Abakumov, without examining these slanderous materials he ordered an investigation of the "affair" of Voznessensky and Kuznetsov. With this, their fate was sealed.

Instructive in the same way is the case of the Mingrelian nationalist organization which supposedly existed in Georgia. As is known, resolutions by the Central Committee, Communist Party of the Soviet Union, were made concerning this case in November 1951 and in March 1952. These resolutions were made without prior discussion with the Political Bureau. Stalin had personally dictated them. They made serious accusations against many loyal Communists. On the basis of falsified documents, it was proven that there existed in Georgia a supposedly nationalistic organization whose objective was the liquidation of the Soviet power in that republic with the help of imperialist powers.

In this connection, a number of responsible party and Soviet workers were arrested in Georgia. As was later proven, this was a slander directed against the Georgian party organization.

We know that there have been at times manifestations of local bourgeois nationalism in Georgia as in several other republics. The question arises: could it be possible that, in the period during which the resolutions referred to above were made, nationalist tendencies grew so much that there was a danger of Georgia's leaving the Soviet Union and joining Turkey? (Animation in the hall, laughter.)

This is, of course, nonsense. It is impossible to imagine how such assumptions could enter anyone's mind. Everyone knows how Georgia has developed economically and culturally under Soviet rule.

Industrial production of the Georgian Republic is 27 times greater than it was before the Revolution. Many new industries have arisen in Georgia which did not exist there before the Revolution: iron smelting, an oil industry, a machine-construction industry, etc. Illiteracy has long since been liquidated, which, in pre-Revolution

Georgia, included 78 per cent of the population.

Could the Georgians, comparing the situation in their republic with the hard situation of the working masses in Turkey, be aspiring to join Turkey? In 1955, Georgia produced 18 times as much steel per person as Turkey. Georgia produces 9 times as much electrical energy per person as Turkey. According to the available 1950 census, 65 per cent of Turkey's total population are illiterate, and, of the women, 80 per cent are illiterate. Georgia has 19 institutions of higher learning which have about 39,000 students; this is 8 times more than in Turkey (for each 1,000 inhabitants). The prosperity of the working people has grown tremendously in Georgia under Soviet rule.

It is clear that, as the economy and culture develop, and as the socialist consciousness of the working masses in Georgia grows, the source from which bourgeois nationalism draws its strength evaporates.

As it developed, there was no nationalistic organization in Georgia. Thousands of innocent people fell victim to wilfulness and lawlessness. All of this happened under the "genial" leadership of Stalin, "the great son of the Georgian nation," as Georgians like to refer to Stalin. (Animation in the hall.)

The wilfulness of Stalin showed itself not only in decisions concerning the internal life of the country but also in the international relations of the Soviet Union.

The July plenum of the Central Committee studied in detail the reasons for the development of conflict with Yugoslavia. It was a shameful role which Stalin played here. The "Yugoslav affair" contained no problems which could not have been solved through party discussions among comrades. There was no significant basis for the development of this "affair"; it was completely possible to gave prevented the rupture of relations with that country. This does not mean, however, that the Yugoslav leaders did not make mistakes or did not have shortcomings. But these mistakes and shortcomings were magnified in a monstrous manner by Stalin, which resulted in a break of relations with a friendly country.

I recall the first days when the conflict between the Soviet Union and Yugoslavia began artifically to be blown up. Once, when I came from Kiev to Moscow, I was invited to visit Stalin, who, pointing to the copy of a letter lately sent to Tito, asked me, "Have you read this?"

Not waiting for my reply, he answered, "I will shake my little finger — and there will be no more Tito. He will fall."

We have dearly paid for this "shaking of the little finger." This statement reflected Stalin's mania for greatness, but he acted just that way: "I will shake my little finger — and there will be no Kossior"; "I will shake my little finger once more and Postyshev and Chubar will be no more"; "I will shake my little finger again — and Voznessensky, Kuznetsov and many others will disappear."

But this did not happen to Tito. No matter how much or how little Stalin shook, not only his little finger but everything else that he could shake, Tito did not fall. Why? The reason was that, in this case of disagreement with the Yugoslav comrades, Tito had behind him a state and a people who had gone through a severe school of fighting for liberty and independence, a people which gave a support to its leaders.

You see to what Stalin's mania for greatness led. He had completely lost consciousness of reality; he demonstrated his suspicion and haughtiness not only in relation to individuals in the USSR, but in relation to whole parties and nations.

We have carefully examined the case of Yugoslavia and have found a proper solution which is approved by the peoples of the Soviet Union and of Yugoslavia as well as by the working masses of all the people's democracies and by all progressive humanity. The liquidation of the abnormal relationship with Yugoslavia was done in the interest of the whole camp of socialism, in the interest of strengthening peace in the whole world.

Let us also recall the "affair of the doctor-plotters."[33] (Animation in the hall.) Actually there was no "affair" outside of the declaration of the woman doctor Timashuk, who was probably influenced or ordered by someone (after all, she was an unofficial collaborator of the organs of state security) to write Stalin a letter in which she declared that doctors were applying supposedly improper methods of medical treatment.

Such a letter was sufficient for Stalin to reach an immediate conclusion that there are doctor-plotters in the Soviet Union. He issued orders to arrest a group of eminent Soviet medical specialists. He personally issued advice on the conduct of the investigation and the method of interrogation of the arrested persons. He said that the academician Vinogradov should be put in chains, another one should be beaten. Present at this Congress as a delegate is the former Minister of State Security, Comrade Ignatiev, Stalin told him curtly.

"If you do not obtain confessions from the doctors we will shorten you by a head." (Tumult in the hall.)

Stalin personally called the investigative judge, gave him instructions, advised him on which investigative methods should be used; these methods were simple — beat, beat and, once again, beat.

Shortly after the doctors were arrested, we members of the Political Bureau received protocols with the doctors' confessions of guilt. After distributing these protocols, Stalin told us,

"You are blind like young kittens; what will happen without me? The country will perish because you do not know how to recognize enemies."

The case was so presented that no-one could verify the facts on which the investigation was based. There was no possibility of trying to verify facts by contacting those who had made the confessions of guilt.

We felt, however, that the case of the arrested doctors was questionable. We knew some of these people personally because they had once treated us. When we examined this "case" after Stalin's death, we found it to be fabricated from beginning to end.

This ignominious "case" was set up by Stalin; he did not, however, have the time in which to bring it to an end (as he conceived that end), and for this reason the doctors are still alive. Now all have been rehabilitated; they are working in the same places they were working before; they treat top individuals, not excluding members of the Government; they have our full confidence; and they execute their duties honestly, as they did before.

In organizing the various dirty and shameful cases, a very base role was played by the rabid enemy of our party, an agent of a foreign intelligence service — Beria, who had stolen into Stalin's confidence. In what way could this *provacateur* gain such a position in the party and in the state, so as to become the First Deputy Chairman of the Council of Ministers of the Soviet Union and a member of the Central Committee of the Political Bureau? It has now been established that this villain had climbed up the Government ladder over an untold number of corpses.

Were there any signs that Beria was an enemy of the party? Yes, there were. Already in 1937, at a Central Committe plenum, former People's Commissar of Health Kaminsky [34] said that Beria worked for the Mussavat intelligence service. But the Central Committee plenum had barely concluded when Kaminsky was arrested and then shot. Had Stalin examined Kaminsky's statement? No, because Stalin believed in Beria, and that was enough for him. And when Stalin believed in anyone or anything, then no one could say anything which was contrary to his opinion; anyone who would dare to express opposition would have met the same fate as Kaminsky.

There were other signs, also. The declaration which Comrade Snegov made to the party's Central Committee is interesting. (Parenthetically speaking, he was also rehabilitated not long ago, after 17 years in prison camps.) In this declaration, Snegov writes:

> "In connection with the proposed rehabilitation of the former Central Committee member, Lavrentiev-Kartvelishvili,[35] I have entrusted to the hands of the representative of the Committee of State Security a detailed deposition concerning Beria's role in the disposition of the Kartvelishvili case and concerning the criminal motives by which Beria was guided.
>
> In my opinion, it is indispensable to recall an important fact pertaining to this case and to communicate it to the Central Committee because I did not consider it as proper to include in the investigation documents.
>
> On October 30, 1931, at the session of the Organizational Bureau of the Central Committee, All-Union Communist Party (Bolsheviks), Kartvelishvili, secretary of the Transcaucasian Krai Committee, made a report. All members of the executive of the Krai Committee were present; of them I alone am alive.
>
> During this session, J.V. Stalin made a motion at the end of his speech concerning the organization of the secretariat of the Transcaucasian Krai Committee composed of the following: first secretary, Kartvelishvili; second secretary, Beria (it was then, for the first time in the party's history, that Beria's name was mentioned as a candidate for a party position). Kartvelishvili answered that he knew Beria well and for that reason refused categorically to work together with him. Stalin proposed then that this matter be left open and that it be solved in the process of the work itself. Two days later a decision was arrived at that

Beria would receive the party post and that Kartvelishvili would be deported from the Transcaucasus."

This fact can be confirmed by Comrades Mikoyan and Kaganovich, who were present at that session.

The long, unfriendly relations between Kartvelishvili and Beria were widely known; they date back to the time when Comrade Sergo[38] was active in the Transcaucasus; Kartvelishvili was the closest assistant of Sergo. The unfriendly relationship impelled Beria to fabricate a "case" against Kartvelishvili. It was a characteristic thing that in this "case" Kartvelishvili was charged with a terroristic act against Beria.

The indictment in the Beria case contains a discussion of his crimes. Some things should, however, be recalled, especially since it is possible that not all delegates to the Congress have read this document. I wish to recall Beria's bestial disposition of the cases of Kedrov,[36] Golubiev, and Golubiev's adopted mother, Baturina — persons who wished to inform the Central Committee concerning Beria's treacherous activity. They were shot without any trial and the sentence was passed *ex post facto,* after the execution.

Here is what the old Communist, Comrade Kedrov, wrote to the Central Committee through Comrade Andreyev[37] (Comrade Andreyev was then a Central Committee secretary):

> "I am calling to you for help from a gloomy cell of the Lefortovsky prison. Let my cry of horror reach your ears; do not remain deaf; take me under your protection; please, help remove the nightmare of interrogations and show that this is all a mistake.
>
> "I suffer innocently. Please believe me. Time will testify to the truth. I am not an agent provocateur of the Tsarist Okhrana; I am not a spy; I am not a member of an anti-Soviet organization of which I am being accused on the basis of denunciations. I am also not guilty of any other crimes against the party and the Government. I am an old Bolshevik, free of any stain; I have honestly fought for almost 40 years in the ranks of the party for the good and prosperity of the nation . . .
>
> " . . . Today I, a 62-year-old man, am being threatened by the investigative judges with more severe, cruel and degrading methods of physical pressure. They (the judges) are no longer capable of becoming aware of their error and of recognizing that their

handling of my case is illegal and impermissible. They try to justify their actions by picturing me as a hardened and raving enemy and are demanding increased repressions. But let the party know that I am innocent and that there is nothing which can turn a loyal son of the party into an enemy, even right up to his last dying breath.

"But I have no way out. I cannot divert from myself the hastily approaching new and powerful blows.

"Everything, however, has its limits. My torture has reached the extreme. My health is broken, my strength and my energy are waning, the end is drawing near. To die in a Soviet prison, branded as a vile traitor to the Fatherland — what can be more monstrous for an honest man? And how monstrous all this is! Unsurpassed bitterness and pain grips my heart. No! No! This will not happen; this cannot be, I cry. Neither the party, nor the Soviet Government, nor the People's Commissar, L.P. Beria, will permit this cruel, irreparable injustice. I am firmly certain that, given a quiet, objective examination, without any foul rantings, without any anger and without the fearful tortures, it would be easy to prove the baselessness of the charges. I believe deeply that truth and justice will triumph. I believe. I believe."

The old Bolshevik, Comrade Kedrov, was found innocent by the Military Collegium. But, despite this, he was shot at Beria's order. (Indignation in the hall.)

Beria also handled cruelly the family of Comrade Ordzhonikidze.[38] Why? Because Ordzhonikidze had tried to prevent Beria from realizing his shameful plans. Beria had cleared from his way all persons who could possibly interfere with him. Ordzhonikdze was always an opponent of Beria, which he told to Stalin. Instead of examining this affair and taking appropriate steps, Stalin allowed the liquidation of Ordzhonikidze's brother and brought Ordzhonikidze himself to such a state that he was forced to shoot himself. (Indignation in the hall.)

Beria was unmasked by the party's Central Committee shortly after Stalin's death. As a result of the particularly detailed legal proceedings, it was established that Beria had committed monstrous crimes and Beria was shot.

The question arises why Beria, who had liquidated tens of thousands of the party and Soviet workers, was not unmasked during Stalin's life. He was not unmasked earlier because he had utilized very skilfully Stalin's weaknesses; feeding him with suspicions, he assisted Stalin in everything and acted with his support.

Comrades: The cult of the individual acquired such monstrous size chiefly because Stalin himself, using all conceivable methods, supported the glorification of his own person. This is supported by numerous facts. One of the most characteristic examples of Stalin's self-glorification and of his lack of even elementary modesty is the edition of his *Short Biography*,[39] which was published in 1948.

This book is an expression of the most dissolute flattery, an example of making a man into a godhead, of transforming him into an infallible sage, "the greatest leader, sublime strategist of all times and nations." Finally, no other words could be found with which to lift Stalin up to the heavens.

We need not give here examples of the loathesome adulation filling this book. All we need to add is that they all were approved and edited by Stalin personally and some of them were added in his own handwriting to the draft text of the book.

What did Stalin consider essential to write into this book? Did he want to cool the ardour of his flatterers who were composing his *Short Biography*? No! He marked the very places where he thought that the praise of his services was insufficient. Here are some examples characterizing Stalin's activity, added in Stalin's own hand:

> "In this fight against the sceptics and capitulators, the Trotskyites, Zinovievites, Bukharinites and Kamenevites, there was definitely welded together after Lenin's death, that leading core of the party ... that upheld the great banner of Lenin, rallied the party behind Lenin's behests, and brought the Soviet people into the broad road of industrializing the country and collectivizing the rural economy. The leader of this core and the guiding force of the party and the state was Comrade Stalin."

Thus writes Stalin himself! Then he adds:

> "Although he performed his task as leader of the party and the people with consummate skill and enjoyed the unreserved support of the entire Soviet people, Stalin never allowed his work to be marred by the slightest hint of vanity, conceit or self-adulation."

Where and when could a leader so praise himself? Is this worthy of a leader of the Marxist-Leninist type? No. Precisely against this did Marx and Engels take such a strong position. This also was always sharply condemned by Vladimir Ilyich Lenin.

In the draft text of his book appeared the following sentence:

"Stalin is the Lenin of today."

This sentence appeared to Stalin to be too weak, so, in his own handwriting, he changed it to read:

"Stalin is the worthy continuer of Lenin's work, or, as it is said in our party, Stalin is the Lenin of today."

You see how well it is said, not by the nation but by Stalin himself. It is possible to give many such self-praising appraisals written into the draft text of that book in Stalin's hand. Especially generously, does he endow himself with praises pertaining to his military genius, to his talent for strategy.

I will cite one more insertion made by Stalin concerning the theme of the Stalinist military genius. He writes:

"The advanced Soviet science of war received further development at Comrade Stalin's hands. Comrade Stalin elaborated the theory of the permanently operating factors that decide the issue of wars, of active defence and the laws of counter-offensive and offensive, of the co-operation of all services and arms in modern warfare, of the role of big tank masses and air forces in modern war and of the artillery as the most formidable of the armed services. At the various stages of the war Stalin's genius found the correct solutions that took account of all the circumstances of the situation." (Movement in the hall.)

And, further writes Stalin:

"Stalin's military mastership was displayed both in defence and offence. Comrade Stalin's genius enabled him to divine the enemy's plans and defeat them. The battles in which Comrade Stalin directed the Soviet armies are brilliant examples of operational military skill."

In this manner was Stalin praised as a strategist. Who did this? Stalin himself, not in his role as a strategist but in the role of an author-editor, one of the main creators of his self-adulatory biography. Such, comrades, are the facts. We should rather say shameful facts.

And one additional fact from the same *Short Biography* of Stalin. As is known, *The Short Course of the History of the All-Union Communist Party (Bolsheviks)* was written by a commission of the party Central Committee.

This book, parenthetically, was also permeated with the cult of the individual and was written by a designated group of authors. This fact was reflected in the following formulation on the proof copy of the *Short Biography* of Stalin:

> "A commission of the Central Committee, All-Union Communist Party (Bolsheviks), under the direction of Comrade Stalin and with his most active personal participation, has prepared a *Short Course of the History of the All-Union Communist Party (Bolsheviks)*."

But even this phrase did not satisfy Stalin: the following sentence replaced it in the final version of the *Short Biography:*

> "In 1938 appeared the book, *History of the All-Union Communist Party (Bolsheviks), Short Course*, written by Comrade Stalin and approved by a commission of the Central Committee, All-Union Communist Party (Bolsheviks)."

Can one add anything more? (Animation in the hall.)

As you see, a surprising metamorphosis changed the work created by a group into a book written by Stalin. It is not necessary to state how and why this metamorphosis took place.

A pertinent question comes to our mind: if Stalin is the author of this book, why did he need to praise the person of Stalin so much and to transform the whole post-October historical period of our glorious Communist party solely into an action of "the Stalin genius"?

Did this book properly reflect the efforts of the party in the socialist transformation of the country, in the construction of socialist society, in the industrialization and collectivization of the country, and also other steps taken by the party which undeviatingly travelled the path outlined by Lenin? The book speaks principally about Stalin, about his speeches, about his reports. Everything without the smallest exception is tied to his name.

And when Stalin himself asserts that he himself wrote the *Short Course of the History of the All-Union Communist Party (Bolsheviks)*, this calls at least for amazement. Can a Marxist-Leninist thus write about himself, praise his own person to the heavens?

Or let us take the matter of the Stalin Prizes. (Movement in the hall.) Not even the Tsars created prizes which they named after themselves.

Stalin recognized as the best a text of the national anthem of the Soviet Union which contains not a word about the Communist party; it contains, however, the following unprecedented praise of Stalin: "Stalin brought us up in loyalty to the people. He inspired us to great toil and acts."

In these lines of the anthem, the whole educational, directional and inspirational activity of the great Leninist party is ascribed to Stalin. This is, of course, a clear deviation from Marxism-Leninism, a clear debasing and belittling of the role of the party. We should add for your information that the Presidium of the Central Committee has already passed a resolution concerning the composition of a new text of the anthem, which will reflect the role of the people and the role of the party. (Loud, prolonged applause.)

And was it without Stalin's knowledge that many of the largest enterprises and towns were named after him? Was it without his knowledge that Stalin monuments were erected in the whole country — these "memorials to the living"? It is a fact that Stalin himself had signed on July 2, 1951, a resolution of the USSR Council of Ministers concerning the erection on the Volga-Don Canal of an impressive monument to Stalin; on September 4 of the same year he issued an order making 33 tons of copper available for the construction of this impressive monument.

Anyone who has visited the Stalingrad area must have seen the huge statue which is being built there, and that on a site which hardly any people frequent. Huge sums were spent to build it at a time when people of this area had lived since the war in huts. Consider, yourself, was Stalin right when he wrote in his biography that

" . . . he did not allow in himself . . . even a shadow of conceit, pride, or self-adoration"?

At the same time Stalin gave proofs of his lack of respect for Lenin's memory. It is not a coincidence that, despite the decision taken over 30 years ago to build a Palace of Soviets as a monument to Vladimir Ilyich, this palace was not built, its construction was always postponed and the project allowed to lapse.

We cannot forget to recall the Soviet Government resolution of August 14, 1925, concerning "the founding of Lenin prizes for educational work." This resolution was published in the press, but until this day there are no Lenin prizes. This, too, should be corrected. (Tumultuous, prolonged applause.)

During Stalin's life — thanks to known methods which I have mentioned, and quoting facts, for instance, from the *Short Biography* of Stalin — all events were explained as if Lenin played only a secondary role, even during the October Socialist Revolution. In many films and in many literary works the figure of Lenin was incorrectly presented and inadmissibly depreciated.

Stalin loved to see the film, *The Unforgettable Year of* 1919, in which he was shown on the steps of an armoured train and where he was practically vanquishing the foe with his own sabre. Let Klimenti Yefremovich[40], our dear friend, find the necessary courage and write the truth about Stalin; after all, he knows how Stalin had fought. It will be difficult for Comrade Voroshilov to undertake this, but it would be good if he did it. Everyone will approve of it, both the people and the party. Even his grandsons will thank him. (Prolonged applause.)

In speaking about the events of the October Revolution and about the Civil War, the impression was created that Stalin always played the main role, as if everywhere and always Stalin had suggested to Lenin what to do and how to do it. However, this is slander of Lenin. (Prolonged applause.)

I will probably not sin against the truth when I say that 99 per cent of the persons present here heard and knew very little about Stalin before the year 1924, while Lenin was known to all; he was known to the whole party, to the whole nation, from the children up to the greybeards. (Tumultuous, prolonged applause.)

All this has to be thoroughly revised so that history, literature and the fine arts properly reflect V.I. Lenin's role and the great deeds of our Communist party and of the Soviet people — the creative people. (Applause.)

Comrades! The cult of the individual has caused the employment of faulty principles in party work and in economic activity; it brought about rude violation of internal party and Soviet democracy, sterile administration, deviations of all sorts, covering up the shortcomings and varnishing of reality. Our nation gave birth to many flatterers and specialists in false optimism and deceit.

We should also not forget that, due to the numerous arrests of party, Soviet and economic leaders, many workers began to work uncertainly, showed over-cautiousness, feared all which was new, feared their own shadows and began to show less initiative in their work.

Take, for instance, party and Soviet resolutions. They were prepared in a routine manner, often without considering the concrete situation. This went so far that party workers, even during the smallest sessions, read their speeches. All this produced the danger of formalizing the party and Soviet work and of bureaucratizing the whole apparatus.

Stalin's reluctance to consider life's realities and the fact that he was not aware of the real state of affairs in the provinces can be illustrated by his direction of agriculture.

All those who interested themselves even a little in the national situation saw the difficult situation in agriculture, but Stalin never even noted it. Did we tell Stalin about this? Yes, we told him, but he did not support us. Why? Because Stalin never travelled anywhere, did not meet city and kolkhoz workers; he did not know the actual situation in the provinces.

He knew the country and agriculture only from films. And these films had dressed up and beautified the existing situation in agriculture. Many films so pictured kolkhoz life that the tables were bending from the weight of turkeys and geese. Evidently, Stalin thought that it was actually so.

Vladimir Ilyich Lenin looked at life differently; he was always close to the people; he used to receive peasant delegates and often spoke at factory gatherings; he used to visit villages and talk with the peasants.

Stalin separated himself from the people and never went anywhere. This lasted ten years. The last time he visited a village was in January 1928, when he visited Siberia in connection with grain deliveries. How then could he have known the situation in the provinces?

And when he was once told during a discussion that our situation on the land was a difficult one and that the situation of cattle breeding and meat production was especially bad, a commission was formed which was charged with the preparation of a resolution called *"Means Toward Further Development of Animal Breeding in Kolkhozes and Sovkhozes."* We worked out this project.

Of course, our proposals of that time did not contain all possibilities, but we did chart ways in which animal breeding on kolkhozes and sovkhozes would be raised. We had proposed then to raise the prices of such products in order to create material incentives for the kolkhoze, MTS[41] and sovkhoz workers in the development of cattle breeding. But our project was not accepted and in February 1953 was laid aside entirely.

What is more, while reviewing this project Stalin proposed that the taxes paid by the kolkhozes and by the kolkhoz workers should be raised by 40 billion rubles; according to him the peasants are well off and the kolkhoz worker would need to sell only one more chicken to pay his tax in full.

Imagine what this meant. Certainly, 40 billion rubles is a sum which the kolkhoz workers did not realize for all the products which they sold to the government. In 1952, for instance, the kolkhozes and the kolkhoz workers received 26,280 million rubles for all their products delivered and sold to the Government.

Did Stalin's position, then, rest on the data of any sort whatever? Of course not. In such cases facts and figures did not interest him. If Stalin said anything, it meant it was so — after all, he was a "genius," and a genius does not need to count, he only needs to look and can immediately tell how it should be. When he expresses his opinion, everyone has to repeat it and to admire his wisdom.

But how much wisdom was contained in the proposal to raise the agricultural tax by 40 billion rubles? None, absolutely none, because the proposal was not based on an actual assessment of the situation but on the fantastic ideas of a person divorced from reality.

We are currently beginning slowly to work our way out of a difficult agricultural situation. The speeches of the delegates to the Twentieth Congress please us all; we are glad that many delegates deliver speeches, that there are conditions for the fulfilment of the sixth Five-Year Plan for animal husbandry, not during the period of five years, but within two to three years. We are certain that the commitments of the new Five-Year Plan will be accomplished successfully. (Prolonged applause.)

Comrades! If we sharply criticize today the cult of the individual which was so widespread during Stalin's life and if we speak about the many negative phenomena generated by this cult which is so alien to the spirit of Marxism-Leninism, various persons may ask: How could it be? Stalin headed the party and the country for 30 years and many victories were gained during his lifetime. Can we deny this? In my opinion, the question can be asked in this manner only by those who are blinded and hopelessly hypnotized by the cult of the individual, only by those who do not understand the essence of the revolution and of the Soviet state, only by those who do not understand, in a Leninist manner, the role of the party and of the nation in the development of the Soviet society.

The Socialist Revolution was attained by the working class and by the poor peasantry with the partial support of middle-class peasants. It was attained by the people under the leadership of the Bolshevik Party. Lenin's great service consisted of the fact that he created a militant party of the working class, but he was armed with Marxist understanding of the laws of social development and with the science of proletarian victory in the fight with capitalism, and he steeled this party in the crucible of revolutionary struggle of the masses of the people.

During this fight the party consistently defended the interests of the people, became its experienced leader, and led the working masses to power, to the creation of the first socialist state. You remember well the wise words of Lenin that the Soviet state is strong because of the awareness of the masses that history is created by the millions and tens of millions of people.

Our historical victories were attained thanks to the organizational work of the party, to the many provincial organizations, and to the self-sacrificing work of our great nation. These victories are the result of the great drive and activity of the nation and of the party as a whole; they are not at all the fruit of the leadership of Stalin, as the situation was pictured during the period of the cult of the individual.

If we are to consider this matter as Marxists and as Leninists, then we have to state unequivocally that the leadership practice which came into being during the last years of Stalin's life became a serious obstacle in the path of Soviet social development. Stalin often failed for months to take up some unusually important problems, concerning the life of the party and of the state, whose solution could not be postponed. During Stalin's leadership our peaceful relations with other nations were often threatened, because one-man decisions could cause, and often did cause, great complications.

In the last years, when we managed to free ourselves of the harmful practice of the cult of the individual and took several proper steps in the sphere of internal and external policies, everyone saw how activity grew before their very eyes, how the creative activity of the broad working masses developed, how favourably all this acted upon the development of economy and of culture. (Applause.)

Some comrades may ask us: Where were the members of the Political Bureau of the Central Committee? Why did they not assert themselves against the cult of the individual in time? And why is this being done only now?

First of all, we have to consider the fact that the members of the Political Bureau viewed these matters in a different way at different times. Initially, many of them backed Stalin actively because Stalin was one of the strongest Marxists and his logic, his strength and his will greatly influenced the cadres and party work.

It is known that Stalin, after Lenin's death, especially during the first years, actively fought for Leninism against the enemies of Leninist theory and against those who deviated. Beginning with Leninist theory, the party, with its Central Committee at the head, started on a great scale the work of socialist industrialization of the country, agricultural collectivization and the cultural revolution.

At that time Stalin gained great popularity, sympathy and support. The party had to fight those who attempted to lead the country away from the correct Leninist path; it had to fight Trotskyites, Zinovievites and rightists, and the bourgeois nationalists. This fight was indispensable.

Later, however, Stalin, abusing his power more and more, began to fight eminent party and Government leaders and to use terroristic methods against honest Soviet people. As we have already shown, Stalin thus handled such eminent party and Government leaders as Kossior, Rudzutak, Eikhe, Postyshev and many others.

Attempts to oppose groundless suspicions and charges resulted in the opponent falling victim of the repression. This characterized the fall of Comrade Postyshev.

In one of his speeches Stalin expressed his dissatisfaction with Postyshev and asked him, "What are you actually?"

Postyshev answered clearly, "I am a Bolshevik, Comrade Stalin, a Bolshevik."

This assertion was at first considered to show a lack of respect for Stalin; later it was considered a harmful act and consequently resulted in Postyshev's annihilation and branding without any reason as a "people's enemy."

In the situation which then prevailed I have talked often with Nikolai Alexandrovich Bulganin; once when we two were travelling in a car, he said, "It has happened sometimes that a man goes to Stalin on his invitation as a friend. And, when he sits with Stalin, he does not know where he will be sent next — home or to jail."

It is clear that such conditions put every member of the Political Bureau in a very difficult situation. And, when we also consider the fact that in the last years the Central Committee plenary sessions were not convened and that the sessions of the Political Bureau occurred only occasionally, from time to time, then we will understand how difficult it was for any member of the Political Bureau to take a stand against one or another unjust or improper procedure, against serious errors and shortcomings in the practices of leadership.

As we have already shown, many decisions were taken either by one person or in a roundabout way, without collective discussion. The sad fate of Political Bureau member Comrade Voznessensky,[42] who fell victim to Stalin's repressions, is known to all. It is a characteristic thing that the decision to remove him from the Political Bureau was never discussed but was reached in a devious fashion. In the same way came the decision concerning the removal of Kuznetsov and Rodionov from their posts.

The importance of the Central Committee's Political Bureau was reduced and its work was disorganized by the creation within the Political Bureau of various commissions — the so-called "quintets," "sextets," "septets" and "novenaries." Here is, for instance, a resolution of the Political Bureau of October 3, 1946:

"Stalin's Proposal:

"1. The Political Bureau Commission for Foreign Affairs ('Sextet') is to concern itself in the future, in addition to foreign affairs, also with matters of internal construction and domestic policy.

"2. The Sextet is to add to its roster the Chairman of the State Commission of Economic Planning of the USSR, Comrade Voznessensky, and is to be known as a Septet.

"Signed: Secretary of the Central Committee, J. Stalin."

What a terminology of a card player! (Laughter in the hall.) It is clear that the creation within the Political Bureau of this type of commissions — "quintets," "sextets," "septets" and "novenaries" — was against the principle of collective leadership. The result of this was that some members of the Political Bureau were in this way kept away from participation in reaching the most important state matters.

One of the oldest members of our party, Klimenti Yefremovich Voroshilov, found himself in an almost impossible situation. For several years he was actually deprived of the right of participation in Political Bureau sessions. Stalin forbade him to attend the Political Bureau sessions and to receive documents. When the Political Bureau was in session and Comrade Voroshilov heard about it, he telephoned each time and asked whether he would be allowed to attend. Sometimes Stalin permitted it, but always showed his dissatisfaction.

Because of his extreme suspicion, Stalin toyed also with the absurd and ridiculous suspicion that Voroshilov was an English agent. (Laughter in the hall.) It's true — an English agent. A special tapping device was installed in his home to listen to what was said there. (Indignation in the hall.)

By unilateral decision, Stalin had also separated one other man from the work of the Political Bureau — Andrei Andreyevich Andreyev. This was one of the most unbridled acts of wilfulness.

Let us consider the first Central Committee plenum after the 19th Party Congress when Stalin, in his talk at the plenum, characterized Vyacheslav Mikhailovich Molotov and Anastas Ivanovich Mikoyan and suggested that these old workers of our party were guilty of some baseless charges. It is not excluded that had Stalin remained at the helm for another several months, Comrades Molotov and Mikoyan would probably have not delivered any speeches at this Congress.

Stalin evidently had plans to finish off the old members of the Political Bureau. He often stated that Political Bureau members should be replaced by new ones.

His proposal, after the 19th Congress, concerning the election of 25 persons to the Central Committee Presidium, was aimed at the removal of the old Political Bureau members and the bringing in of less experienced persons so that these would extol him in all sorts of ways.

We can assume that this was also a design for the future annihilation of the old Political Bureau members and, in this way, a cover for all shameful acts of Stalin, acts which we are now considering.

Comrades! In order not to repeat errors of the past, the Central Committee has declared itself resolutely against the cult of the individual. We consider that Stalin was excessively extolled. However, in the past Stalin doubtless performed great services to the party, to the working class and to the international workers' movement.

This question is complicated by the fact that all this which we have just discussed was done during Stalin's life under his leadership and with his concurrence; here Stalin was convinced that this was necessary for the defence of the interests of the working classes against the plotting of enemies and against the attack of the imperialist class.

He saw this from the position of the interest of the working class, of the interest of the labouring people, of the interest of the victory of socialism and communism. We cannot say that these were the deeds of a giddy despot. He considered that this should be done in the interest of the party, of the working masses, in the name of the defence of the revolution's gains. In this lies the whole tragedy!

Comrades! Lenin had often stressed that modesty is an absolutely integral part of a real Bolshevik. Lenin himself was the living personification of the greatest modesty. We cannot say that we have been following this Leninist example in all respects.

It is enough to point out that many towns, factories and industrial enterprises, kolkhozes and sovkhozes, Soviet institutions and cultural institutions have been referred to by us with a title — if I may express it so — of private property of the names of these or those Government or party leaders who were still active and in good health. Many of us participated in the action of assigning our names to various towns, rayons, enterprises and kolkhozes. We must correct this. (Applause.)

But this should be done calmly and slowly. The Central Committee will discuss this matter and consider it carefully in order to prevent errors and excesses. I can remember how the Ukraine learned about Kossior's arrest. The Kiev radio used to start its programmes thus: "This is Radio (in the name of) Kossior." When one day the programmes began without naming Kossior, everyone was quite certain that something had happened to Kossior, that he probably had been arrested.

Thus, if today we begin to remove the signs everywhere and to change names, people will think that these comrades in whose honour the given enterprises, kolkhozes or cities are named also met some bad fate and that they have also been arrested. (Animation in the hall.)

How is the authority and the importance of this or that leader judged? On the basis of how many towns, industrial enterprises and factories, kolkhozes and sovkhozes carry his name. Is it not about time that we eliminate this "private property" and "nationalize" the factories, the industrial enterprises, the kolkhozes and the sovkhozes? (Laughter, applause, voices: "That is right.") This will benefit our cause. After all, the cult of the individual is manifested also in this way.

We should, in all seriousness, consider the question of the cult of the individual. We cannot let this matter get out of the party, especially not to the press. It is for this reason that we are considering it here at a closed Congress session. We should know the limits; we should not give ammunition to the enemy; we should not wash our dirty linen before their eyes. I think that the delegates to the Congress will understand and assess properly all these proposals. (Tumultuous applause.)

Comrades! We must abolish the cult of the individual decisively, once and for all; we must draw the proper conclusions concerning both ideological-theoretical and practical work. It is necessary for this purpose:

First, in a Bolshevik manner to condemn and to eradicate the cult of the individual as alien to Marxism-Leninism and not consonant with the principles of party leadership and the norms of party life, and to fight inexorably all attempts at bringing back this practice in one form or another.

To return to and actually practice in all our ideological work the most important theses of Marxist-Leninist science about the people as the creator of history and as the creator of all material and spiritual good of humanity, about the decisive role of the Marxist party in the revolutionary fight for the transformation of society, about the victory of communism.

In this connection we will be forced to do much work in order to examine critically from the Marxist-Leninist viewpoint and to correct the widely spread erroneous views connected with the cult of the individual in the sphere of history, philosophy, econony and of other sciences, as well as in literature and the fine arts. It is especially necessary that in the immediate future we compile a serious textbook of the history of our party which will be edited in accordance with scientific Marxist objectivism, a textbook of the history of Soviet society, a book pertaining to the events of the Civil War and the Great Patriotic War.

Secondly, to continue systematically and consistently the work done by the party's Central Committee during the last years, a work characterized by minute observation in all party organizations, from the bottom to the top, of the Leninist principles of party leadership, characterized, above all, by the main principle of collective leadership, characterized by the observance of the norms of party life described in the statutes of our party, and, finally, characterized by the wide practice of criticism and self-criticism.

Thirdly, to restore completely the Leninist principles of Soviet socialist democracy, expressed in the Constitution of the Soviet Union, to fight wilfulness of individuals abusing their power. The evil caused by acts violating revolutionary socialist legality which have accumulated during a long time as a result of the negative influence of the cult of the individual has to be completely corrected.

Comrades! The 20th Congress of the Communist Party of the Soviet Union has manifested with a new strength the unshakable unity of our party, its cohesiveness around the Central Committee, its resolute will to accomplish the great task of building communism. (Tumultuous applause.)

And the fact that we present in all their ramifications the basic problems of overcoming the cult of the individual which is alien to

Marxism-Leninism, as well as the problem of liquidating its burdensome consequences, is an evidence of the great moral and political strength of our party. (Prolonged applause.)

We are absolutely certain that our party, armed with the historical resolutions of the 20th Congress, will lead the Soviet people along the Leninist path to new successes, to new victories. (Tumultuous prolonged applause.)

Long live the victorious banner of our party —Leninism! (Tumultuous, prolonged applause ending in ovation. All rise.)

FOOTNOTES

1. The interesting letter to Wilhelm Bloss which Khrushchev cites was not readily available to students of Marx during Stalin's time. It does not feature in the "only edition authorised by the Marx-Engels-Lenin Institute" of the selected correspondence of Marx and Engels. This collection was translated into English and published by Martin Lawrence in 1934. It has frequently been reissued since.
2. Nadezhda Konstantinovna Krupskaya: Lenin's wife, who worked in the Commissariat for Education after the Revolution. Her memoire skates over her political fears, shared with her husband, during the period between 1921 and 1923. After Lenin's death, she tried to have his "testament" read out to the delegates of the Thirteenth Congress of the CPSU(B), but this was over-ruled by the Central Committee. She subsequently became deputy commissar for education in the Russian republic, and died in 1939.
3. Lev Borisovich Kamenev: together with Grigory Zinoviev was a constant confidant and valued aide of Lenin between 1908 and 1914. After their vacillations during the days before the Revolution, chronicled by Khrushchev later in this text, Kamenev became president of the Moscow Soviet and editor of Lenin's works. Zinoviev became president of the Comintern. Both formed a "troika" with Stalin after Lenin's death, primarily directed against Trotsky. Quickly came into conflict with Stalin, and then joined forces with Trotsky. "Capitulated" to Stalin after the 15th Congress (December 1927). Expelled from the Party in 1932, were readmitted before the 17th Congress in 1934, and then were imprisoned in connection with the assassination of Sergei Mironovich Kirov, Central figures on the first 'Moscow Trial' of August 1936. Executed. (See *Makers of the Russian Revolution*, by Georges Haupt and Jean-Jacques Marie, (Allen and Unwin, 1974).
4. Grigory Zinoviev: see note 3 on Kamenev.
5. Seventeenth Congress of the CPSU(B) was held on 26 January - 10 February 1934: most of Stalin's opponents of the left and right oppositions had publicly recanted and many appeared to record their conversion in its proceedings. The assassination of Kirov, however, which followed, became the pretext for a wave of repressions which crushed almost all former oppositionists.

6. Trotskyites: a generic term used for followers of L.D. Trotsky, but also applied by Stalin (and his successors) to a wide variety of dissenters who did not always subscribe to Trotsky's political ideas. Trotsky was deported from the USSR in 1929, and murdered by a Soviet agent in Mexico, in 1940. An outstanding biography exists: Isaac Deutscher: *The Prophet Armed, The Prophet Unarmed,* and *The Prophet Outcast.* (Oxford University Press.)

7. Bukharinites: the "Right opposition", led by Nicolai Ivanovich Bukharin, was indispensible to Stalin in his battle with the Left oppositionists, culminating in 1928 with their final defeat. Immediately after the routing of the Left, Stalin began a change of policy, and attacked his erstwhile allies on the right. Most prominent supporters of this group besides Bukharin were Rykov (President of the Council of People's Commissars) and Tomsky, the trade union leader. Having been isolated and forced to recant by Stalin, Bukharin was given various responsibilities, including the editorship of *Isvestia* and a place on the committee which drafted the present Soviet Constitution. Arrested and brought to the third great show trial in March 1938, both Bukharin and Rykov were executed. Tomsky had already committed suicide. An imported recent biography of Bukharin is by Stephen Cohen (published by Wildwood House).

8. Rodzianko: former chamberlain to the tsar, subsequently president of the Duma after the February Revolution.

9. The Socialist Revolutionaries (S-Rs) a party formed from several currents within the late nineteenth century Narodnik movement, during 1902. Basing themselves upon the peasantry, their chief platform was for the socialisation of the land. From their Narodnik origins they maintained a predisposition to terroristic politics, involving assassinations and other acts of personal violence. The party split after the February revolution of 1917. Part of it joined Kerensky's provisional government, while part of it was subsequently allied with the Bolsheviks on the October rising.

10. Lavrenti Beria: Stalin's final security chief, succeeding to the post held previously by Yagoda and Yezhov, both of whom perished in the purges which they themselves conducted. Beria was summarily shot, and posthumously accused of having been a foreign agent. Khrushchev repeats some of these accusations in this indictment. No evidence has been offered on this particular score, although there is a great deal of evidence that Beria was indeed an evil person. See, in particular, Roy Medvedev: *Let History Judge* (Spokesman Books).

11. The New Economic Policy: developed after the tenth party Congress, from 8-16 March 1921, extended a wide area of market relationships, in contradistinction from previous rule of "war communism" with its policies of requisitions and equality of scarcity. See E.H. Carr: *The Bolshevik Revolution, 1917-23,* Volume II, chapter xix. (MacMillan, Penguin Books). See also Day: *Leon Trotsky and the Politics of Economic Isolation:* Cambridge University Press, 1973.

12. The Eighteenth Congress of the CPSU(B) was held on 10-21 March 1939. At it Khrushchev made a speech which is frequently ironically counterposed to the one which forms the bulk of this volume. The Nineteenth Congress, which dropped the title (Bolshevik) from the Party's name, was held on 5-14 October 1952. Stalin confined himself to a very short intervention.

13. Sergei Mironovich Kirov, murdered on 1 December 1934, was widely thought of as Stalin's heir-apparent. After the February 1917 Revolution he became prominent on the joint Bolshevik-Menshevik organisation in Caucasia: as a delegate to the Vladicaucasian Soviet after September 1917 he became close to Ordzhonikidze. The first Party Congress he attended was the tenth in 1921: from then on he became part of Stalin's circle. He was head of the Leningrad organisation when he was assassinated, and was also one of four secretaries of the Central Committee.

Explanatory Notes

His death has been described as "the beginning of a coup d'etat". It is widely thought that Stalin had a hand in covering up, if not actually arranging, his murder, which became the pretext for all the subsequent public show trials. See Medvedev's *Let History Judge* for a balanced discussion of these issues.

14. Abel Yenukidze: an active supporter of Stalin in the late 'twenties, this worker-militant (who had pioneered socialist organisation in the Caucasus) fell foul of Beria and was expelled from the Party in June 1935. He was tried clandestinely and shot on 20 December 1937.

15. Andrei Zhdanov: Stalin's close aide, in charge of Leningrad up to his death in 1948, Zhdanov was accorded a role as "theoretician". His edicts on cultural affairs (1946-7), denouncing such eminent Soviet writers as Akhmatova and Zoschenko, and criticising the composers Prokofiev and Shostakovich, became a symbol for all that was uncouth in the doctrines of "socialist realism". His death became the pretext for another purge, since a group of Jewish doctors were accused of plotting his murder.

16. M.M. Kaganovich: played a major role in Stalin's drive to exterminate communist cadres, carefully set out in *Let History Judge*. Dismissed from the leadership in 1957 after an abortive coup against Khrushchev, and named as a member of an "anti-party group". Other members of this group were named as Molotov, Malenkov, and, in a subordinate role, Shepilov.

17. V.M. Molotov: a former Menshevik, became, under Stalin, both prime minister and then foreign secretary. Although he did not escape his master's threats, and his wife was held for some time under close arrest, Molotov was himself a tireless instigator of the repression. See also *Let History Judge*.

18. N.I. Yezhov: Appointed NKVD Commission in place of Yagoda on 25 September 1936. Gave his name to the most frenzied period of the purge, the "Yezhovschina", in which millions were deported and vast numbers died. Subsequently liquidated in 1940. "Was fated to play one of the most shameful and frightful roles in the history of the country, indeed in the history of the world" says Roy Medvedev in *Let History Judge*.

19. G.G. Yagoda: head of the NKVD prior to Yezhov's appointment: tried in 1938 alongside Bukharin, and executed.

20. General Denikin: leader of the white armies operating on the Southern front and in the Ukraine during the Civil War.

21. Felix Dzerzhinsky: a militant in the Polish and Lithuanian socialist movements, Dzerzhinsky joined the Bolsheviks in 1917. In December 1917 founded the *Cheka*, the forerunner of the GPU. Died of a heart attack at a Central Committee meeting in 1926.

22. P.P. Postyshev: Secretary of the Ukrainian Central Committee until 1937, Postyshev took an active part in Stalin's repression, even after his wife was arrested. Demoted, and then shot, in 1938.

23. R.I. Eikhe: "sanctioned many arrests of so-called Trotskyites and Bukharites, who were forced to bear false witness against Eikhe, with the result that he was shot as the leader of the Trotskyite-Bukharinite underground in West Siberia." Roy Medvedev: *Let History Judge*, p.406.

24. V.I. Mezhlauk: former chairman of Gosplan, the state planning commission. Shot just after completing a paper in "Planning and ways to improve it".

25. I.E. Rudzutak: chairman of the planning committee on chemical production. Arrested at his dacha where he was entertaining some famous painters (including Gerasimor) at the time. Shot.

26. Stanislav Kossior: a pole, took an active part in the Revolution in Petrograd, fought in the Ukraine, and was elected to the central committee of the party in the Ukraine. Although his brother supported Trotsky,

he was a supporter of Stalin, although he was aligned with Kirov. Was demoted from first secretaryship of the Ukraine in 1938, and shot without trial in 1939. The leadership of the Polish Communist Party were also executed.

27. Vlas Yakovlevich Chubar: a tough organiser who was charged by Lenin with the economic revival of the Urals in 1919; who took over the problems of the Ukraine in 1920, and who replaced Rakovsky as head of the Ukraine's government in 1923. A firm supporter of Stalin's, he became all-Union Minister of Finance in 1937 and was shot in 1939.

28. A. Kosarev: the Stalinist Komsomol leader, was denounced as an enemy by the Komsomol Central Committee, and arrested some time afterwards. Although he then died, it was rumoured that he had been 'seen' in Moscow after his posthumous rehabilitation by Khrushchev.

29. Kuzma Kryuchkov: pseudonym of pre-revolutionary Russian satirist.

30. A.N. Poskrebyshev. Stalin's personal secretary, was married to Trotsky's son's wife's sister "but that did not prevent (him) from being one of the closest people to Stalin" (Medvedev). His wife was finally arrested, but he escaped such treatment.

31. The "Leningrad Affair". Thousands of arrests were ordered in Leningrad between 1949 and 51. The leaders of the Gosplan were tried, and some were shot. Beria and Malenkov played an active part in this repression.

32. V.S. Abakumov: head of Smersh during the war, minister of State Security between 1946 and 1951. Brought to public trial for "falsifying the Leningrad Case" and sentenced to death. Two of Abakumov's colleagues, Komarov and Likhachev, also tried with him, helped organise the fake trials in Budapest, Sofia and Prague between 1949 and 1952. The trial of Slansky and others in Prague still awaits satisfactory revision by the Czechoslovak authorities, even though it was being undertaken at an accelerated pace by the Dubcek administration before the 1968 invasion. Abakumov and his co-conspirators were sentenced in December 1954!

33. The doctors' plot was "unmasked" three months after the Nineteenth Congress. Nine "terrorist" doctors had confessed to murdering Zhdanov. Seven of these were jews. Two died in captivity, but seven of the nine were released after Stalin's death when the "plot" was officially repudiated. Khrushchev's suggestion that the plot was directed at Molotov, Mikoyan and Voroshilov has also been augmented by the suggestion (Shapiro: *History of the CPSU*, pp.543-4) that Beria might have been among the targets. Two pieces of circumstantial evidence support this contention: no-one accused Beria of participating in the frame-up of the doctors when he was posthumously charged with a variety of offences: and Stalin had conducted a purge of Mingrelians, all close to Beria, just before his death.

34. G.N. Kaminsky had been secretary of the Azerbaijan Central Committee, and Chairman of the Baku Soviet, in 1922.

35. Lavrenti Kartvelishvili: this case is documented in full in Medvedev: *Let History Judge*, pp.241 et seq.

36. M.S. Kedrov: an old Bolshevik and OGPU official, retired by 1939, who had known damaging facts about Beria in 1921. He and his son Igor, also a NKVD operative, wrote to Stalin warning against Beria's appointment to the post of Commissar for Internal Affairs, in early 1939. Igor was immediately shot, and his father soon followed him. Cf. Medvedev, *Let History Judge*, pp.246 et seq.

37. A.A. Andreyev, a Central Committee Secretary: "a man who played no small part in Stalin's machine of mass terror" (*Let History Judge*, p.247).

38. Sergo Ordzhonikidze: old Bolshevik, was elevated by Stalin to preside over the Party Central Control Commission in November 1926. Charged with the expulsion of first the left, and then the right, oppositions, he became reluctant to prosecute this with the required enthusiasm. In

spite of this, he was promoted Commissar for heavy industry in 1932 with Piatakov as his deputy (who did all the work). Beria's rise menaced Ordzhonikidze, and the deposition of Kartvelishvili was followed by the execution of Piatakov after the November 1936 trial, in which he was a defendant. After several members of his family were arrested, Ordzhonikidze was alleged to have committed suicide, in circumstances which remain profoundly suspicious.

39. *Joseph Stalin: A Short Biography,* was compiled by G.F. Alexandrov, M.R. Galaktionov, V.S. Kruzhkov, M.B. Mitin, V.D. Mochalov, P.N. Pospelov. Published in the Soviet Union in 1947, an English edition was brought out in 1949.

40. Klimenti Yefremovich Voroshilov: as a main source of legend about Stalin's military prowess in the civil war, Voroshilov, who was subsequently to be named as a member of the "anti-party group" would have found these remarks difficult to swallow.

41. Machine Tractor Stations had been designed not only to service the collective farms with modern technology, but also to serve as instruments of political and social control. But their political departments co-existed with regional and local party organisations, soviet executives, and ministerial bodies; with the result that confusion became widespread. In September 1953 the political departments of the MTS were abolished, and political supervision of the collective forms became the sole responsibility of district party organs. If anything, though, the organisational-productive responsibilities of MTS were thereby increased. The MTS were finally abolished altogether in 1958.

42. N.A. Voznessenksy: promoted very quickly during the early 'forties, Voznessensky became a member of the politbureau, and deputy chairman of the Council of Ministers. Chairman of Gosplan from December 1937. His book on the War Economy of the USSR was published in 1947, and was said to have provoked Stalin's jealousy. An English edition was issued by the Moscow Foreign Languages Publishing House (1948). Was shot in 1950.

Eighteeen Documents were circulated as an addendum to N.S. Khrushchev's Special Report. Six of these had appeared previously in various forms in publications outside the USSR, but twelve of them had never before been published.

Documents
Published as an addendum to N. S. Khrushchev's Special Report

3

Documents

1   **LETTER TO THE CONGRESS**

I should very much like to advise that a series of changes in our political organisation be undertaken at this Congress.

I should like to share with you those thoughts which I consider to be most essential.

I submit, as of primary importance, that the size of the C.C. membership is enlarged to several dozen, possibly even to one hundred members. It seems to me that our Central Committee would be exposed to great danger in case future developments would not be favourable to us (and we cannot rely on it) — if we had not undertaken such a reform.

Next, I would like to call the Congress' attention to the proposal that under some conditions Gosplan resolutions should be given a legislative character, taking into consideration here Com. Trotsky's proposition — up to a certain point and under certain conditions.

Referring to the first point, i.e. enlargement of the C.C. membership, I am of the opinion that it is necessary for the raising of C.C. authority and for the serious work aimed at raising the efficiency of our apparatus, as also for the prevention of conflicts between small C.C. groupings which would gravely affect the fate of the party as a whole.

I think that our party has the right to demand fifty to 100 C.C. members from the working class whom it can give up without taxing its strength too highly.

This reform would lay the foundation for a greater stability of our party and would help it in its struggle in the encirclement of hostile nations, a struggle which in my opinion can and must greatly sharpen in the next few years. I think that thanks to such a move the stability of our party would increase a thousandfold.

23 XII '22   LENIN.
Taken down by M.V.

Additions to Letter to the Congress: 24 and 25 December, 1922
December 30, 1922

2   LENIN'S 'TESTAMENT'

By the stability of the Central Committee, of which I spoke before, I mean measures to prevent a split, so far as such measures can be taken. For, of course, the White Guard in *Russkaya Mysl* (I think it was S.E. Oldenburg) was right when, in the first place, in his play against Soviet Russia he banked on the hope of a split in our party, and when, in the second place, he banked for that split on serious disagreements in our party.

Our party rests upon two classes, and for that reason its instability is possible, and if there cannot exist an agreement between those classes its fall is inevitable. In such an event it would be useless to take any measures or in general to discuss the stability of our Central Committee. In such an event no measures would prove capable of preventing a split. But I trust that is too remote a future, and too improbable an event, to talk about.

I have in mind stability as a guarantee against a split in the near future, and I intended to examine here a series of considerations of a purely personal character.

I think that the fundamental factor in the matter of stability — from this point of view — is such members of the Central Committee as Stalin and Trotsky. The relation between them constitutes, in my opinion, a big half of the danger of that split, which might be avoided, and the avoidance of which might be promoted, in my opinion, by raising the number of members of the Central Committee to fifty or one hundred.

Comrade Stalin, having become General Secretary, has concentrated an enormous power in his hands; and I am not sure that he always knows how to use that power with sufficient caution. On the other hand, Comrade Trotsky, as was proved by his struggle against the Central Committee in connection with the question of the People's Commissariat of Ways and Communications, is distinguished not only by his exceptional abilities — personally he is, to be sure, the most able man in the present Central Committee — but also by his too far-reaching self-confidence and a disposition to be too much attracted by the purely administrative side of affairs.

These two qualities of the two most able leaders of the present Central Committee might, quite innocently, lead to a split; if our party does not take measures to prevent it, a split might arise unexpectedly.

I will not further characterize the other members of the Central Committee as to their personal qualities. I will only remind you that the October episode of Zinoviev and Kamenev was not, of course, accidental, but that it ought as little to be used against them personally as the non-Bolshevism of Trotsky.

Of the younger members of the Central Committee, I want to say a few words about Bukharin and Pyatakov. They are in my opinion, the most able forces (among the youngest) and in regard to them it is necessary to bear in mind the following: Bukharin is not only the most valuable and biggest theoretician in the party, but also may legitimately be considered the favourite of the whole party; but his theoretical views can only with the very greatest doubt be regarded as fully Marxist, for there is something scholastic in him (he never has learned, and I think never has fully understood, the dialectic).

And then Pyatakov — a man undoubtedly distinguished in will and ability, but too much given over to administration and the administrative side of things to be relied on in a serious political question.

Of course, both these remarks are made by me merely with a view to the present time, or supposing that these two able and loyal workers may not find an occasion to supplement their knowledge and correct their one-sidedness.

December 25, 1922.

Postscript: Stalin is too rude, and this fault, entirely supportable in relations among us Communists, becomes insupportable in the office of General Secretary. Therefore, I propose to the comrades to find a way to remove Stalin from that position and appoint to it another man who in all respects differs from Stalin only in superiority — namely, more patient, more loyal, more polite and more attentive to comrades, less capricious, etc. This circumstance may seem an insignificant trifle, but I think that from the point of view of preventing a split and from the point of view of the relation between Stalin and Trotsky which I discussed above, it is not a trifle, or it is such a trifle as many acquire a decisive significance.

January 4, 1923   LENIN

Continuation of notes: 26 December, 1922

3   ENLARGING THE CENTRAL COMMITTEE

The enlargement of the C.C. membership to fifty or even 100 persons would serve, as I see it, a two- or three-fold purpose; the more C.C. members there are, the more persons will get to know the C.C. work and the smaller will be the danger of a split as a result of taking some careless step. Enlistment of many workers into the C.C. will help our workers improve the efficiency of our apparatus, which is very bad.

Actually we have inherited it from the old regime, because it was entirely impossible for us to reorganise it completely in such a short time, especially during the period of war, or famine, etc. For that reason the "critics", who, in a derogatory or sarcastic manner, point out the defects of our apparatus, can be boldly answered that they have no conception whatever of the conditions of our present revolution.

Effective reorganisation of the apparatus within five years was entirely impossible — especially during the period of the revolution. It is enough that during five years we managed to create a government of a new type in which the workers at the head of the peasants stand against the bourgeoisie, and this at the time when we are encircled by a hostile world; this was a tremendous accomplishment. This should not blind us, however, to the fact that it is actually the old apparatus which we have taken over, the apparatus of the Czar and the bourgeoisie.

And that now, when we have attained peace and have satisfied our minimal needs, we should devote all our efforts toward improving the efficiency of the apparatus. I picture this to myself in this manner; several dozen workers taken into the C.C. machinery will be more able than anyone else to occupy themselves with the control, efficiency and transformation of our apparatus.

It became evident that the workers-peasants inspection which initially possessed this function is incapable of performing it and can be used only as an "auxiliary", or, under some conditions, as an assistant of these C.C. members. Workers drawn into the C.C. should, in my opinion, not be recruited from among those who have behind them a long period of service in the Soviet apparatus (in this part of my letter I count the peasants as workers in every case — because these workers have acquired certain habits and certain prejudices, which we specifically consider it necessary to combat).

The C.C. staff should be enlisted largely from among the workers who are below the level of the group which were promoted during the last five years to positions in the Soviet apparatus, and who are close to the common workers and peasants, who are not directly or indirectly in the category of the exploiters. I think that such workers, not attending all C.C. meetings and all Politbureau meetings, and having the opportunity to read all C.C. documents — are capable of creating the cadre of loyal supporters of the Soviet system; they will be able also, firstly, to add to the stability of the C.C. itself, and secondly, to work actually on rebuilding the apparatus and making it efficient.

Taken down by L.F.
26 XII '22

Continuation of notes: 27 December, 1922
4   CONCERNING THE ASSIGNMENT OF LEGISLATIVE
    FUNCTIONS TO THE STATE PLANNING COMMISSION

This was, it seems to me, first put forward by Com. Trotsky. I opposed it, because I considered that in such a case this would introduce a basic inconsistency into the system of our legislative institutions. After a thorough examination of this question, I have nevertheless come to the conclusion that it contains an essentially healthy idea, namely that Gosplan is somewhat divorced from our legislative institutions despite the fact that, being an assembly of competent individuals, experts and representatives of science and technology, it actually has the most data necessary to assess the situation.

Until now, however, our viewpoint was that Gosplan should deliver to the State carefully compiled materials sufficient for State institutions to decide the affairs of the State. I consider that in the present situation, when government affairs have become unusually complicated, when it is continuously necessary to decide on questions which require the expert knowledge of Gosplan members and occasionally on questions which do not require such expert knowledge, and, what is more, when it is necessary to decide on questions, parts of which do and parts of which do not require such expert knowledge of Gosplan — I consider that at the present time we have to take the step to broaden Gosplan's powers.

I picture to myself this step as follows: Gosplan's decisions cannot be put aside by the regular governmental processes, but require special procedures such as the presentation of the matter before a V.Ts.I.K. session, its preparation in accordance with special instructions, accompanied by special regulations and notes necessary for consideration of whether a given Gosplan decision should be abrogated and finally — the review of Gosplan's decisions should be made at regular and specific intervals, etc.

Com. Trotsky's concurrence in this matter, in my opinion, could and should be obtained, but not as to the assignment to the post of Gosplan chairman of one of our political leaders or the chairman of the Supreme Council of National Economy, etc. It seems to me that in this question the basic consideration is much too closely tied up with personal considerations. It seems to me that the concurrently expressed objections to the chairman of Gosplan, Krizhanovsky, and his deputy, Piatakov, are two-fold.

On the one hand, they are criticised on the grounds that they are too easy-going, that they do not assert themselves, that they lack character, and, on the other hand, that they are supposedly too uncouth, that they behave like first sergeants, that they do not have a sufficiently solid scientific background, etc. It seems to me that these criticisms encompass two sides of the question pushed to their extremes and that we do need in Gosplan the skilful combination of both of these types, one represented by Piatakov, and the other by Krizhanovsky.

In my opinion Gosplan should be headed by a man with scientific background, specifically in technology or agriculture, a man with great practical experience, an experience of several dozen years in the field of technology or agriculture. In my opinion such a man needs not so much administrative ability as he needs wide experience and the ability to lead.

27 XII '22   LENIN
Taken down by M.V.

5   Continuation of the letter on the legislative character of Gosplan
28 XII '22

I have noted that some of our comrades, who are in positions to effect the affairs of the state in a decisive manner, over-emphasise the administrative side of the question, which at the proper time and place is, of course, indispensable, but which, however, should not be erroneously equated with scientific knowledge, with the capacity for comprehension of broad realities, with leadership, talent, etc.

Every government institution, and specifically Gosplan, requires the happy combination of these two qualities; thus, when Com. Krizkanovsky told me that he managed to get Piatakov for the work in Gosplan and that there was a meeting of minds as to the division of labour — I, giving my consent, felt, deep in me, on the one side, certain doubts, but visualised, on the other hand, that we might realise the desired combination of the two types of governmental leaders.

When my hope was realised — to assess this, we must wait awhile; we must, over a period of time, check this in practice; in principle, however — I think — we cannot doubt that the proper functioning of governmental institutions absolutely requires such a combination of characters and types (men, qualities). In my opinion, in this case, the exaggeration of "administrativeness" is just as harmful as exaggeration generally.

A director of a governmental institution should possess in the highest degree the capacity for leadership and a solid scientific and technical knowledge to the extent needed for checking a person's work. This is essential. Without it, no real work can be done. On the other hand, he has to know how to administer and has to have for this purpose a suitable assistant or even assistants. It is doubtful whether we will find the combination of these two qualities in one person; it is equally doubtful whether such a combination is necessary.

Taken down by L.F.   LENIN
28 XII '22

6   Continuation of the notes: 29 December, 1922

Gosplan, it appears, is being completely transformed into a commission of experts. At the head of this institution there should be a man of great and broad scientific attainments in the field of technology. Administrative ability should be here only a useful adjunct. Gosplan doubtlessly needs to be to a certain degree independent and self-governing provided only that the employees of this institution are honest and honestly seek to carry out our plan of economic and social construction.

The last quality, is found today, of course, only in unique cases, because the overwhelming majority of scientists, of which Gosplan is naturally made up, is heavily burdened with bourgeois views and pre-conceptions. To control these people in this respect should be the task of several individuals who can constitute a Gosplan presidium; these individuals should be Communists and should be checking daily, during the progress of the work, to what degree the bourgeois scientists are devoted to the cause, whether they are unburdening themselves of their bourgeois prejudices, and also whether they are gradually accepting the Socialist point of view. This two-fold activity — scientific control coupled with purely administrative work — is the ideal to which Gosplan leaders in the new republic should aspire.

Is it logical to chop up the work done by Gosplan into individual directives, or — on the other hand — should we aim at the creation of a permanent band of specialists who would be subject to systematic control by the Gosplan presidium, who could reach decisions as to the entirety of the problems within the scope of Gosplan's activity? In my judgment, the second of the two is more logical and we should make an effort to limit the number of burning and important specific problems.

Taken down by M.V.   LENIN
20 XII '22

Continuation of the Notes: 29 December, 1922
7   FOR THE CHAPTER ON RAISING THE NUMBER OF C.C. MEMBERS

When raising the number of C.C. members, it is necessary, in my opinion, to solve — probably first of all — the problem of control and efficiency of our apparatus, which is good for nothing. For this purpose we should utilise the services of highly qualified specialists; the task of making these specialists available belongs to the workers-peasants inspection.

How the work of these control specialists, who also have sufficient knowledge, is to be co-ordinated with the work of these new C.C. members — practice should decide. It appears to me that the workers-peasants inspection (as the result of its development and also as the result of doubts in regard to this development) has reached a stage, which we now observe, namely, a stage of transition from a separate people's commissariat to the assignment of special function to C.C. members. This transition is away from an institution which inspects absolutely everything — away from a group consisting only of a few members who are, however, first class inspectors who have to be well-paid (this is particularly indispensable in our era, when everything has to be paid for and in the situation when the inspectors are employed only in the institutions which offer better pay.)

If the number of C.C. members is adequately raised and if they attend each year a course on administration of governmental affairs, benefiting from the help of the highly qualified specialists and of members of the workers-peasants inspection, who are highly authoritative in every sphere of activity — then, I think we will successfully solve this problem which has so long evaded solution.

Therefore, totally: about 100 C.C. members and no more than 400-500 assistants, who, in their capacity as members of the workers-peasants inspection, control in accordance with their directives.

29 December 1922 LENIN
Taken down by M.V.

8   MEMORANDUM TO MEMBERS OF THE PARTY C.C./R.C.P.

Proletarians of all Countries, Unite!
The Communist Party (Bolshevik) of Russia.
The Central Committee
Department of the Bureau of the Secretariat

No. 12644 16 April, 1923

TO ALL MEMBERS OF THE C.C./R.C.P.

On order of Com. Stalin there are sent for the information of C.C. members:-

a) Letter of Com. Trotsky to the C.C. members;
b) Articles of Com. Lenin on the national question, written at the end of December, 1922;
c) A letter of Com. Fotiyeva to Com. Kamenev together with his answer;
d) A letter of Com. Fotiyeva to Com. Stalin;
e) Com. Stalin's declaration.

Assistant to the C.C. Secretary, U. Azaretyan.

9   LETTER FROM TROTSKY TO STALIN AND MEMBERS OF THE C.C./R.C.P.

a) To Com. Stalin. To All Members of the C.C./R.C.P.

I have today received the enclosed copy of a letter from the personal secretary of Com. Lenin, Com. Fotiyeva, to Com. Kamenev concerning an article of Com. Lenin about the national question.

I had received Com. Lenin's article on 5th March together with three notes of Com. Lenin, copies of which are also enclosed.

I had made at that time a copy of this article, as a document of particularly basic significance and have used it as the basis for my corrections (accepted by Com. Stalin) of Com. Stalin's theses, as well as for my own article on the national question published in *Pravda*.

This article, as already stated, is of singularly basic significance. It contains also a sharp condemnation of three C.C. members. As long as even a shadow of hope existed that Vladimir Ilyich had left some instruction concerning this article for the party congress, for which it was obviously meant, judging by all signs and especially by Com. Fotiyeva's note — so long have I avoided bringing this article up.

In the situation, which has now arisen — as is also evident from Com. Fotiyeva's letter — I have no alternative but to make this article known to the Central Committee members, because, in my opinion, this article has no lesser significance from the viewpoint of party policy on the national question than the former article on the question of the relationship between the proletariat and the peasantry.

If — on the basis of motives of an inner-party nature, whose significant is self-evident — no C.C. member will make this article in one form or another known to the party or to the party congress, I, on my part will consider this as a decision of silence, a decision which — in connection with the party congress — removes from me personal responsibility for this article.

16 IV '23
No. 90/T
Enclosures: Com. Fotiyeva's letter, three notes and an article of Com. Lenin.

                                              L. TROTSKY

Received at 8.10 p.m. 16. IV '23.
For accuracy: E. Lepeshinskaya.

10 CONCERNING THE NATIONAL QUESTION OF AUTONOMISATION".

I have committed, I think, a great offence against the workers of Russia because I have not pressed with sufficient energy and sharpness the well-known autonomisation question, known officially, it seems to me, as the question of the union of the Soviet Socialist Republics.

In the summer, when this question arose, I was ill, and then in the autumn I was too confident of my recovery and believed that I could press this matter at the October and December plenums. However, I could not attend either the October plenum, devoted to this problem or the December plenum; and in this way this question passed me by almost entirely.

I managed only to talk with Com. Dzherzhinsky, who had returned from the Caucasus, and who related to me how this question looks in Georgia. I also managed to exchange a few words with Com. Zinoviev and passed on to him my anxiety concerning this question. What I heard from Com. Dzherzhinsky, who was at the head of commission sent by the Central Committee for the purpose of "investigating" the Georgia incident, made me expect nothing but the worst. If things have gone so far that Ordzonikidze could stoop to using physical violence, which was told me by Com. Dzherzhinsky, then it can be imagined in what a quagmire we have landed. Evidently the whole concept of "autonomisation" was basically wrong and inopportune.

It is said that we need the unity of the apparatus. Whence came these assurances? Was it not from the same Russian apparatus, which, as I have already noted in one of the earlier numbers of my journal, we have taken over from the Czarate and have only thinly annointed with the Soviet holy oil?

It cannot be doubted that we should have waited with this matter until we could have said that we answer for the apparatus as for our very own. And now we should conscientiously say something quite the opposite, namely, that we call as our own an apparatus, which is really foreign to us and which is a bourgeois and Czarist hodge-podge, which we had no chance of subduing during the past five years without the help of our states under conditions when the "business" of war and the fight against the famine was more important.

Under such conditions it is an entirely natural thing that the point about the "freedom to withdraw from the union", with which we justify to ourselves, will prove to be but a scrap of paper, insufficient for the defence of foreign races in Russia against the inroads of that very generically Russian man, the Great Russian, the chauvinist, and actually a villain and a ravager, which is what the typical Russian bureaucrat is. It cannot be doubted but that the insignificant percentage of Soviet and Sovietised workers will drown in this chauvinistic sea of Great Russian rascality like a fly in the milk.

It is offered in the defence of this undertaking that the people's commissariats whose activity includes the matters pertaining to the national spirit, national education, are autonomous. But a question arises here whether it is possible to keep the people's commissariats entirely unrelated to the centre and also a second question, whether we have applied measures with proper care for the purpose of defending foreign races against the generically, the typically, Russian Derzhimorda (after a character in a novel by Gogol, noted for his brutal arrogance). In my judgment we have not taken such measures although we could and should have done so.

I think that a fatal role was played here by hurry and the administrative impetuousness of Stalin and also his infatuation with the renowned "social-nationalism". Infatuation in politics generally and usually plays the worst role.

I am also afraid that Com. Dzherzhinsky, who went to the Caucasus in order to investigate the "crimes" of these "social-nationalists" distinguished himself also by his typically Russian disposition (it is a common knowledge that Russified members of other nationalities always like to exaggerate when it comes to typically Russian attitudes): the objectivity of his whole commission is characterised by Ordzhonikidze's "accomplishments". In my opinion, no provocation and also no insults can justify these Russian good deeds and that Com. Dzherzhinsky has committed an irreparable offence by treating these deeds frivolously.

To all other citizens of the Caucasusm Ordzhonikidze was the government. Ordzhonikidze had no right to allow himself such impulsiveness as that with which he and Dzherzhinsky have tried to excuse themselves. Quite on the contrary, Ordzhonikidze was duty-bound to show self-control to a degree that is not obligatory for other plain citizens, let alone a citizen charged with "political" crime. After all the "social-nationalists" were actually citizens charged with a political crime and all circumstances of this accusation could only thus describe it.

Here we are already approaching a very basic question: what should we understand by internationalism.

December 30, 1922   LENIN

Continuation of Notes: 31 December, 1922
Concerning the National Question of "Autonomisation".

I have already written in my works creating the national question, that an abstract conception of nationalism is absolutely worthless. Distinction should be made between the nationalism of an oppressing nation, the nationalism of a large nation and the nationalism of a small nation.

Speaking about the second type of nationalism, we, the nationals of a great nation, show ourselves almost always in historical practice guilty of untold numbers of outrages and, what is more — we do not even observe that we are perpetrating untold numbers of acts of violence and abuse; it should suffice for me to cite my own Volga recollections to show with what contempt we treated non-Russians; a Pole is always referred to as "Polak", a Tartar is sarcastically called a "Count", a Ukrainian — a "Kohkol", a Georgian and other members of the Caucasian nations — a "Capcasian man".

For this reason the internationalism of the oppressing nation, or of the so-called "Great" nation (even if it is great only through its own violence, great only as an overlord can be "great") should depend not only on the formal observation of equality among nations, but also of such inequality by which the oppressing nation, the large nation, would compensate for that inequality which actually exists in life. He who does not understand this does not understand the true proletarian approach to the national question, actually, still retains the petty bourgeois outlook and, for that reason, cannot but fall into the bourgeois position.

What is important to a proletarian? For a proletarian it is not only important but essential and compelling that other nationalities offer him the maximum of trust in the proletarian class struggle.

What is the pre-requisite for this? More than a formal equality is required. It is required that he compensate, in one way or another, through his behaviour towards, or through his concessions to, the other nationalities for that distrust, that suspicion, those grievances which they have experienced in the historical past at the hands of the government of the "big-power" nation.

I should think that the Bolsheviks and Communists need no further explanation. I think that in the case before us, the case of the Georgian nation, we have a typical example in which a really proletarian approach requires of us a special caution, understanding and making of concessions. A Georgian who treats this side of the matter with frivolity, who frivolously chatters about the charges of "social-nationalism" (while he himself is not only a real and authentic "social-nationalist" but also a brutal Great Russian Derzhimorda), that Georgian actually harms the interests of proletarian class solidarity, because nothing so much impedes the development and strengthening of proletarian class solidarity as national injustice; the oppressed nationals are not as sensitive in regard to any other matter as in regard to their equality and, in regard to non-observance of this equality by the proletarian comrades even when this is due only to negligence or is demonstrated in the form of a joke. It is for this reason that in this case it would be preferable to sin by too much rather than too little concession and indulgence towards national minorities.

It is for this reason that the basic interest of proletarian solidarity and, therefore, of the proletarian class-struggle, demands in this case that we never treat the national question in a formal manner, but that we always take into account the indispensable difference which should exist in the relationship of the proletarian oppressed (or small) nation with the oppressing (or large) nation.

31 XII '22   LENIN
For accuracy: Lepeshinskaya

Continuation of the notes: 31st December, 1922
Concerning the National Question of "Autonomisation".

What practical measures should be taken in the situation which has developed?

Firstly, we should retain and strengthen the Union of Socialist Republics; there can be no doubt about this. We need this as the Communist proletariat of the whole world needs it in the fight with the international bourgeoisie and in the defence against its machinations.

Secondly, we should retain the Union of Socialist Republics in regard to the diplomatic apparatus. It should be mentioned here that this apparatus is quite exceptional in the governmental apparatus. We excluded everyone from the old Czarist apparatus who formerly had even the slightest influence. Here, the whole apparatus, possessing the slightest influence, was made up of Communists. For this reason this apparatus has acquired for itself (we can boldly say) the name of a Communist apparatus which has been tested and cleansed of the old Czarist bourgeois and petty bourgeois influence to a degree incomparably higher than that attained in the apparatus with which we have had to be satisfied in the other people's commissariats.

Thirdly, Comrade Ordzhonikidze has to be punished as an example. (I say this with regret, the more so because I myself belong to the circle of his friends and have worked with him abroad, in the emigration). It is necessary also to examine again or anew all the materials of the Dzherzhinsky commission in order to correct that great mass of injustices and of biased judgments definitely contained in them. Political responsibility for this whole truly Great Russian nationalistic campaign should be placed squarely on the backs of Stalin and Dzherzhinsky.

Fourthly, we should introduce the most vigorous rules concerning the use of the national language in the republics of other nations which are members of our union; and we should insure that most meticulous observance of these rules. There is no doubt that under the pretext of unity of railway service, under the pretext of fiscal unity, etc., a great number of abuses of the essentially Russian type will be experienced by us. To fight these abuses we must practice an exceptional vigilance; this is in addition to the special integrity required of those who will devote themselves to this fight.

We will need here a detailed code which can be compiled, even if only imperfectly, only by the nationals residing in a given republic. It should not be predetermined that, while we do this, we will nevertheless not consider at the next congress of Soviets the return to the former situation, i.e. that we will retain the Union of the

Socialist Soviet Republics only in the sphere of military affairs and diplomacy, while in other matters each of the people's commissariats will be fully independent.

We should keep in mind that the split of the people's commissariats and the lack of co-ordination of their work in relation to Moscow and to other centres can be overcome to a sufficient degree with the authority of the party provided this authority is used with a more or less satisfactory circumspection and impartiality. The harm to our state which could result from lack of unity of the national apparatuses with the Russian apparatus would be incomparably smaller, infinitely smaller, than that other harm to us and also to the whole international, to the hundreds of millions of the nations of Asia, who, treading in our footsteps, are expected in the nearest future to appear on the stage of history.

It would be unforgivable opportunism if we, on the eve of this emergence of the East and in the dawn of its awakening, would undermine in its eyes our authority even through the smallest tactlessness towards and injustice against our own members of other races. The necessity of solidarity against the imperialism of the West, which is defending the capitalist world, is a different matter. Here, there is no doubt and I need not say that I praise these measures without any qualification. It is another thing, however, when we see that we ourselves generate an imperialistic outlook on relations with the oppressed nationalities, even if it concerns only insignificant points; this undermines completely our whole principled sincerity and our whole principled defence of the fight against imperialism. And the day of tomorrow in the history of the world will be precisely that day when the people oppressed by imperialism will awaken and when the decisive, long and hard fight for their liberation will begin.

31 XII '22 LENIN
For accuracy: Lepeshinskaya

11 CONFIDENTIAL LETTER FROM LENIN TO TROTSKY
Copy from a copy for eyes only.

TOP SECRET

Dear Com. Trotsky,

I ask you urgently to undertake the defence of the Georgia case in the C.C. of the party. This case is at present "being shot at" by Stalin and Dzherzhinsky and I cannot count on their objectivity. Even to the contrary. If you would agree to undertake the defence of that case, I would be at ease. If you could not for some reason agree to do this, please return to me all the materials. This will be for me the sign of your refusal.

Hearty party greetings.

Written by M.V. LENIN
5 March, '23
For accuracy: M. Volodichevan.

12 NOTE FROM LENIN'S SECRETARY TO TROTSKY

To Comrade Trotsky,

Vladimir Ilyich asked me that, in addition to the letter whose content you were given by telephone, I informed you that Com. Kamenev is going to Georgia on Wednesday; V.I. wants to know if you would not want to send there something from yourself.

5 March, '23 M. Volodicheva.

13 THE LETTER OF COM. FOTIYEVA TO COM. KAMENEV
Copy to Com. Trotsky

Lev Borisovich,

I am transmitting to you, as the active chairman of the Political

Bureau, the following which is pertinent to our telephone conversation.

As I have already informed you on 31, XII, '22, Vladimir Ilyich had dictated an article concerning the nationality question.

He was very interested in this question and was preparing himself to present this question at the party congress.

Shortly before his last illness he informed me that he would publish this article, but later, after that, he took ill and made no final arrangements.

V.I. considered his article as a document of guidance and attached great importance to it. On the order of Vladimir Ilyich this article was transmitted to Com. Trotsky to whom V.I. entrusted the defence of his position on this question at the party congress because they have both held identical views in this matter.

The only copy of this article which I have is preserved at V.I.'s order is in his secret archive.

I am transmitting this for your information.

I was unable to do it earlier because I have only today returned to work after a period of illness.

16 IV '23
For accuracy: E. Lepeshinskaya

Personal Secretary to Com. Lenin,
L. FOTIYEVA

14   ACKNOWLEDGEMENT BY KAMENEV OF FOTIYEVA'S LETTER
Answer of Com. Kamenev to the C.C. Secretariat

Only a moment ago, at 35 minutes after 5, I received the enclosed note from Com. Fotiyeva. I am sending this note to the C.C. because it contains nothing which pertains to me personally. In my opinion the C.C. should immediately decide affirmatively the question of publishing the article of Vladimir Ilyich.

For correctness: E. Lepeshinskaya   L. KAMENEV
16 IV '23. 5.45

15 LETTER OF FOTIYEVA TO STALIN
The Letter of Com. Fotiyeva.

Com. Stalin,

I have today sought the advice of Mariya Ilyinishna in the question whether Vladimir Ilyich's article which I sent to you should be published because of the fact that Vladimir Ilyich had expressed the intent to publish it in connection with a speech which he intended to make at the congress.

Mariya Ilyinishna has expressed the opinion that this article should not be printed because V.I. had not issued a clear order concerning its publication; she only grants the possibility of making this article known to the delegates to this congress.

From my own point of view I need only to add that V.I. did not consider this article to be in its final form and ready for the printer.

16 IV '22   L. FOTIYEVA
9 o'clock in the evening.

16 THE DECLARATION OF COM. STALIN TRANSMITTED TO C.C. MEMBERS

I am greatly surprised that the articles of Com. Lenin, which, without a doubt are of a distinct basic significance, and which Com. Trotsky had received already on 5 March of this year — he considers admissible to keep as his own secret for over a month without making their content known to the Political Bureau or to the C.C. plenum, until one day before the opening of the twelfth congress of the party. The theme of these articles — as I was informed today by the congress delegates — are subject to discussion and rumours and stories among the delegates; these articles, as I have learned today, are known to people who have nothing in common with the C.C.; the C.C. members themselves must seek information from these rumours and stories, while it is self-evident that the content of these articles should have been reported first of all to the C.C.

I think that Com. Lenin's article should be published in the press. It is only regrettable that — as is clearly evident from Com. Fotiyeva's letter — these articles apparently cannot be published because they have not been reviewed by Com. Lenin.

10 o'clock p.m.   J. STALIN
16 IV '23.

17   PROTOCOL BY N.K. KRUPSKAYA FOR THE EXCLUSIVE USE OF PARTY ORGANISATIONS

I have transmitted the notes which V. Ilyich dictated to me during his illness from 23 December to 23 January — 13 separate notes. This total number does not yet include the note concerning the national question (Mariya Ilyinishna has it). Some of these notes have already been published (on the workers-peasants inspection and on Sukhanov). Among the unpublished notes are those of 24-25 December, 1922, and those of 4 January, 1923, which contain personal characterisations of some C.C. members. Vladimir Ilyich expressed the definite wish that this note of his be submitted after his death to the next party congress for its information.

N. KRUPSKAYA

The documents mentioned in the declaration of Com. N.K. Krupskaya, which are to be transmitted to the C.C. plenum commission, were received by me on 18 May, 1924.

L. KAMENEV

(Lenin died 21 January, 1924. The XIIIth Congress of the Russian Communist Party — Bolsheviks — took place from 23-31 May, 1924.)

Vladimir Ilyich's notes mentioned above and transmitted to Com. Kamenev — are all known to me and were earmarked by Vladimir Ilyich for transmittal to the party.

18 V, '24   K. KRUPSKAYA
End of protocol

18 NOTE OF C.C. PLENUM COMMISSION

Having familiarised itself with the documents which were transmitted to Com. Kamenev by N.K. Krupskaya on 18.V.'24 the C.C. plenum decided:

To submit them to the nearest party congress for its information.

19. V. '24

G. ZINOVIEV
A. SMIRNOV
M. KALININ
N. BUKHARIN
J. STALIN
L. KAMENEV

23 XII '22

The following resolution was approved by the Central Committee of the C.P.S.U. on 30 June, 1956.

A Resolution of the Central Committee of the C.P.S.U.

A Resolution

30th June 1956

I

The Central Committee of the Communist Party of the Soviet Union notes with satisfaction that the historic 20th Congress of the CPSU has been welcomed entirely and supported wholeheartedly by our party as a whole, by the entire Soviet people, by the fraternal Communist and Workers' parties, by working people of the great community of socialist nations, and by millions of people in the capitalist and colonial countries. And this is quite understandable, for the 20th Party Congress, marking as it did a new stage in the creative development of Marxism-Leninism, gave a thorough-going analysis of the present international situation both at home and in the world, equipped the Communist Party and the Soviet people as a whole with a magnificent plan for the continued effort for building Communism, and opened up new prospects for united action of all working-class parties in averting the danger of war, and on behalf of the interests of labour.

The Soviet people, carrying out the decisions of the 20th Congress, are gaining more and more outstanding achievements in every aspect of the country's political, economic and cultural life under the leadership of the Communist Party. The Soviet people have rallied still more closely behind the Communist Party and are showing a wealth of constructive initiative in their efforts to accomplish the tasks set before them by the 20th Congress.

The period which has passed since the Congress was held has shown also the great and vital importance of its decisions for the international Communist and labour movement, for the struggle of all progressive forces to strengthen world peace. The important theoretical theses the Congress laid down on the peaceful coexistence of states with different social systems, on the possibility of preventing wars in modern times, on the multiplicity of forms of the transition of nations to socialism, are having a favourable effect on the international situation, promoting the relaxation of tension, greater unity of action of all the forces working for peace and democracy, and the strengthening of the positions of the world socialist system.

While the Soviet people and the working people of the people's democracies and of the world as a whole have met the historic decisions of the 20th Congress of the CPSU with great enthusiasm and with a new upsurge of constructive initiative and revolutionary energy, they have caused alarm and irritation in the camp of the enemies of the working class. Reactionary circles in the United States and in some other capitalist powers obviously feel uneasy about the great programme to strengthen peace which the 20th Congress of the CPSU has charted. Their uneasiness increases as this programme is being put into operation, vigorously and consistently.

Why are the enemies of Communism and socialism making most of their attacks on the shortcomings about which the Central Committee of our party told the 20th Congress of the CPSU? The reason they are doing so is to divert the attention of the working class and its parties from the main issues which were raised at the 20th Party Congress and which were meant to clear the way to further progress being made in the cause of peace, socialism and working-class unity.

The decisions of the 20th Party Congress and the foreign and home policy of the Soviet government have created confusion in imperialist quarters in the United States and some other countries.

The bold and consistent foreign policy of the USSR, directed towards ensuring peace and co-operation between nations regardless of their social systems, is winning support from the great masses of the people in all countries of the world extending the front of peace-loving nations and causing a profound crisis in the cold war policy, a policy of building up military blocs and stockpiling arms. It is no accident that it is the imperialist elements in the United States that have been making the greatest fuss over the efforts made in the USSR to combat the cult of the individual. The existence of negative factors arising from the cult of the individual was profitable for them in order to fight socialism with these facts at their disposal. Now that our party is boldly overcoming the consequences of the cult of the individual, the imperialists see in it a factor making for our country's faster progress towards Communism, and weakening the positions of capitalism.

The ideologists of capitalism, in an effort to undermine the great power of attraction of the decisions of the 20th Congress of the CPSU and their influence on the broadest masses of the people, are resorting to all manner of tricks and ruses to distract the attention of the working people from the progressive and inspiring ideas the socialist world puts forward before humanity.

The bourgeois press has lately launched a large-scale campaign of anti-Soviet slander, which the reactionary circles are trying to justify by some of the facts connected with the cult of the individual of J.V. Stalin denounced by the Communist Party of the Soviet Union. The sponsors of this campaign are exerting every effort to "trouble the waters", to conceal the fact that what is meant is a stage the Soviet Union has passed through in its development; they are out to suppress and misrepresent the fact that in the years that have passed since Stalin's death the Communist Party of the Soviet Union and the Soviet government have been acting with exceptional perseverance and resolution to remove the after-effects of the cult of the individual, and have been making steady progress in solving new problems for the sake of strengthening peace, and building Communism, in the interest of the people at large.

Bourgeois ideologists, in launching their campaign of slander, are trying to cast a slur once more, and again to no avail, on the great ideas of Marxism-Leninism, to shake the trust the working people have in the world's first socialist country — the USSR — and to sow confusion in the ranks of their international Communist and labour movement.

Historical experience indicates that the opponents of international proletarian unity have in the past attempted more than once to take advantage of what they believed to be opportune moments for undermining the international unity of the Communist and Workers' parties, for dividing the international labour movement, for weakening the forces of socialism. But each time the Communist and Workers' parties have discerned the intrigues of the enemies of socialism, have rallied their ranks still more closely, demonstrating their unshakeable political unity, and their unbreakable loyalty to the ideas of Marxism-Leninism.

The fraternal Communist and Workers' parties have detected this move of the enemies of socialism in good time, too, and are giving it a fitting rebuff. It would be incorrect, on the other hand, to shut one's eyes to the fact that some of our friends abroad are still not quite clear on the cult of the individual and its consequences and are sometimes giving incorrect interpretations to some of the points connected with the cult of the individual.

The party bases its criticism of the cult of the individual on the principles of Marxism-Leninism. For over three years our party has been waging a constant fight against the cult of the person of J.V. Stalin, and persistently overcoming its harmful consequences. It is only natural that this question should have entered as an important item into the deliberations of the 20th Congress of the CPSU and its decisions. The Congress recognised that the Central Committee had taken perfectly correct and timely action against the cult of the individual which, as long as it was widespread, belittled the role of the party and the masses, whittled down the role of collective leadership in the party and often led to serious omissions in its work, and to gross violation of socialist law. The congress instructed the Central Committee to carry out consistently the measures for removing wholly and entirely the cult of the individual, foreign to Marxism-Leninism, for removing its consequences in every aspect of party, governmental and ideological activity, and for strict enforcement of the standards of party life and of the principles of collective party leadership elaborated by the great Lenin.

In combating the cult of the individual the party guides itself by the well-known theses of Marxism-Leninism on the role of the masses, of parties and individuals in history, and on the impermissibility of a cult of the person of a political leader, however great his merits may be. Karl Marx, the founder of scientific Communism, emphasising his revulsion for "any cult of the individual", declared that he and Friedrich Engels joined the Association of Communists "on condition that everything making for superstitious worshipping of authorities would be thrown out of it". (*Karl Marx and Friedrich Engels, Works,* Vol. 26, First Russian Edition, pp. 487-8.)

In building up our Communist Party, V.I. Lenin was irreconcilable in fighting the anti-Marxist conception of the "hero" and the "mob", emphatically denouncing the counter-posing of individual heroes to the masses of the people. "The intellect of scores of millions," said V.I. Lenin, "creates something immeasurably higher than a forecast of the greatest genius." (*Works,* Vol. 26, p. 431.

In raising the question of combating the cult of the person of J.V. Stalin, the Central Committee of the CPSU acted on the assumption that the cult of the individual contradicted the essence of the socialist system and was becoming a brake on the way of progress of Soviet democracy and of the advance of Soviet society towards Communism.

The 20th Congress of the party, on the Central Committee's initiative, found it necessary to speak openly and boldly about the grave consequences of the cult of the individual, of the serious mistakes made in the latter period of Stalin's life, and to appeal to the party as a whole to put an end, through combined efforts, to everything that the cult of the individual had brought in its train. In doing so the Central Committee realised that the frank admission of the errors made would give rise to certain negative features and excesses which the enemies could use. The bold and ruthless self-criticism in matters arising from the cult of the individual has been fresh, ample evidence of the strength and vitality of our party and of the Soviet socialist system. It can be said with confidence that none of the ruling parties in capitalist countries would ever have ventured to do anything like this. Quite the reverse; they would have tried to pass over in silence and to hide from the people facts as unpleasant as these. But the Communist Party of the Soviet Union, reared as it is on the revolutionary principles of Marxism-Leninism, has spoken the whole truth, however bitter it might have been. The party took this step on its own initiative, guiding itself by consideration of principle. It is believed that even if its action against the Stalin cult caused some momentary difficulties, it would be of enormous value in the long run from the point of view of the basic interests and ultimate goals of the working class. Sure guarantees are thereby created against things like the cult of the individual reappearing in our party or in our country ever again, and also for the leadership of the party and the country being effected collectively, through enforcing the Marxist-Leninist policy, in conditions of full-scale party democracy, with the active and constructive participation of millions of working people and with the utmost development of Soviet democracy.

By taking a determined stand against the cult of the individual and its consequences, and by openly criticising the errors it caused, the party has once more demonstrated its loyalty to the immortal principles of Marxism-Leninism, its loyalty to the interests of the people, its concern for providing the best possible conditions for the development of party and Soviet democracy in the interest of the successful building of Communism in this country. The Central Committee of the CPSU places on record the fact that the discussions on the cult of the individual and its consequences by party organizations and at general meetings of working people have been marked by a great measure of activity, shown both by the party membership and by non-party people, and that the CPSU Central Committee's line has been welcomed and supported wholly and entirely both by the party and by the people.

The facts of the violations of socialist law and other errors connected with the cult of the individual of J.V. Stalin, which the party has made public, naturally create a feeling of bitterness and deep regret. But the Soviet people realize that the condemnation of the cult of the individual was indispensable for the building of Communism in which they are all playing their full part. The Soviet people have seen the party taking persistent practical steps for the past few years to remove the after-effects of the cult of the individual in every field of party, governmental, economic and cultural development. Thanks to this effort, the party, which no longer has its internal forces bound by anything, has drawn still closer to the people and has today developed its creative activity more than ever before.

II

How, indeed, could it happen that the cult of the person of Stalin, with all the attendant adverse consequences, could have appeared and gained currency in conditions of the Soviet system?

This question should be examined against the background of the objective, concrete historical conditions under which socialism was built in the USSR, and also some subjective factors arising from Stalin's personal qualities.

The October Socialist Revolution has gone down in history as a classic example of a revolutionary transformation of capitalist society under the leadership of the working class. The example of the heroic struggle of the Bolshevik Party, of the world's first socialist state, the USSR, is something from which the Communist parties of other lands, indeed all progressive and democratic forces, are learning how to solve the fundamental social problems generated by modern social development. Throughout the nearly forty years that have gone into building socialist society, the working people of this country have accumulated a wealth of experience, which is being studied and assimilated by the working people of other socialist nations, creatively and in keeping with their specific conditions.

This was the first experience history has ever known of building a socialist society which was taking shape through the quest for and practical proving of many truths which until then were known to socialists only in general outline, theoretically. For over a quarter of a century the Soviet Union was the only country blazing the path to socialism for mankind. It was like a besieged fortress in capitalist encirclement. The enemies of the Soviet Union, both in the West and in the East, continued to plot new "crusades" against the USSR after the failure of the 14-power intervention of 1918-20. The enemies sent large numbers of spies and wreckers into the USSR, trying by every means at their disposal to destroy the world's first socialist state. The threat of renewed imperialist aggression against the USSR increased particularly after fascism's advent to power in Germany in 1933, which proclaimed its purpose to be that of destroying Communism, that of destroying the Soviet Union, the world's first state of working people. Everyone remembers the establishment of what was called the "anti-Comintern pact" and the "Berlin-Rome-Tokyo axis", which were actively supported by the forces of international reaction as a whole. With a threat of a new war growing more and more evident, and with the western powers cold-shouldering the measures the Soviet Union more than once proposed to put fascism in a straitjacket and organize collective security, the Soviet Union had to exert every effort for strengthening its defences and countering the intrigues of the hostile capitalist encirclement. The party had to teach the people as a whole to be always vigilant and prepared to face enemies from without.

The intrigues of international reaction were all the more dangerous since there was a bitter class struggle going on within the country for a long time to see "who beats whom?" After Lenin's death, hostile trends began gaining currency in the party: Trotskyites, right-wing opportunists and bourgeois nationalists whose stand was one of opposition to Lenin's theory about the possibility of the victory of socialism in one country, a stand which would in fact have led to the restoration of capitalism in the USSR. The party launched a ruthless struggle against those enemies of Leninism.

In carrying out Lenin's behests, the Communist Party steered a course towards the country's socialist industrialization, collectivizing agriculture and making a cultural revolution. The Soviet people and the Communist Party have had to overcome unimaginable difficulties and obstacles in solving these supreme problems of building a socialist society in a single country. Our country had to overcome its age-old backwardness and re-shape the national economy as a whole along new, socialist lines, within the historically shortest period of time, and without any economic assistance whatsoever from outside.

This complicated international and internal situation called for iron discipline, tireless enhancement of vigilance, stringent centralization of leadership, which could not but have had an adverse effect on the development of some democratic forms. In the bitter struggle against the whole world of imperialism our country had to accept some limitations to democracy, which were justified logically by our people's struggle for socialism in conditions of capitalist encirclement.

But even at that time the party and the people regarded these limitations as temporary and due to be removed as the strength of the Soviet state grew and the forces of democracy and peace developed throughout the world. The people made these temporary sacrifices conscientiously, seeing the Soviet social system make progress day by day.

All these difficulties on the way to socialism have been overcome by the Soviet people under the leadership of the Communist Party and its Central Committee, which consistently pursued Lenin's general line.

The victory of socialism in this country, faced as it was with hostile encirclement and the ever-present threat of attack from without, was an historic exploit of the Soviet people. Through carrying out its first Five-Year Plans, the economically backward country made a giant leap ahead in its economic and cultural development, thanks to the strenuous and heroic efforts of the people and the party. With the progress achieved in socialist construction the living standards of the working people were raised and unemployment abolished once and for all. A thorough cultural revolution took place. Within a short space of time the Soviet people produced great numbers of technicians who rose to the level of world technological progress and brought Soviet science and technology to one of the leading places in the world. It was the great party of Communists that was the inspiring and organizing force behind these victories. By the example of the USSR the working people of the whole world have seen for themselves that the workers and peasants, once they have taken power into their own hands, can build and develop successfully, without any capitalists and landowners, their own socialist state, representing and defending the interests of the people at large. All this has played a great and inspiring role in increasing the influence of the Communist and Workers' parties in all the countries of the world.

J.V. Stalin, who held the post of General Secretary of the party's Central Committee for a long period, worked actively in common with other leaders of the party to put into effect Lenin's behests. He was faithful to Marxism-Leninism, and as a theorist and an organizer of high calibre he led the party's fight against the Trotskyites, right-wing opportunists, and bourgeois nationalists, against the intrigues of capitalists from without. It was in this political and ideological fight that Stalin earned great authority and popularity. But there was a mistaken practice of associating all our great victories with his name. The achievements gained by the Communist Party and by the Soviet Union, the eulogies of Stalin made him dizzy. That being the situation, the cult of the person of Stalin was being gradually built up.

Some of J.V. Stalin's individual qualities, which were regarded as negative yet by V.I. Lenin, contributed in great measure to building up the cult of the individual. Towards the end of 1922 Lenin said in a letter to the coming party Congress:

"Comrade Stalin, after taking over the post of General Secretary, accumulated in his hands immeasurable power, and I am not certain whether he will be always able to use this power with the required care." In addition to this letter, writing early in January 1923, V.I. Lenin reverted to some of Stalin's individual qualities, intolerable in a leader. "Stalin is excessively rude," Lenin wrote, "and this defect, which can be freely tolerated in our midst and in contacts among us, Communists, becomes a defect which cannot be tolerated in one holding the post of General Secretary. I therefore propose to the comrades to consider the method by which to remove Stalin from his post, and to select another man for it who, above all, would differ from Stalin in only one quality, namely, greater tolerance, greater loyalty, greater politeness and a more considerate attitude towards the comrades, a less capricious temper, etc."

These letters of Lenin's were brought to the knowledge of the delegations to the 13th Party Congress which met soon after Lenin died. After discussing these documents it was recognized as desirable to leave Stalin in the position of General Secretary on the understanding, however, that he would heed the critical remarks of V.I. Lenin and draw all the proper conclusions from them.

Having retained the post of General Secretary of the Central Committee, Stalin did take into account the critical remarks of Vladimir Ilyich during the period immediately following his death. Later on, however, Stalin, having overestimated his own merits beyond all measure, came to believe in his own infallibility. He began transferring some of the limitations on party and Soviet democracy, unavoidable in conditions of a bitter struggle against the class enemy and its agents, and subsequently during the war against the Nazi invaders, into the standards of party and governmental life, grossly flouting the Leninist principles of leadership. Plenary meetings of the Central Committee and Congresses of the party were held irregularly and later were not held at all for many years. Stalin, in fact, was above criticism.

Great harm to the cause of socialist construction, and the development of democracy inside the party and the state was caused by Stalin's erroneous formula alleging that, with the advance of the Soviet Union to socialism, the class struggle would grow increasingly sharp. This formula, which is true only for certain stages of the transition period, when the question of "who will win?" was being decided, when a persistent class struggle for the construction of the foundations of socialism was proceeding, was advanced to the foreground in 1937, at a time when socialism had already triumphed in our country, when the exploiting classes and their economic base had been eliminated. In practice, this erroneous theoretical formula was used to justify gross violations of socialist law and mass repressions.

It is precisely in these conditions that, among other things, a special status was created for the state security organs, which enjoyed tremendous trust because they had rendered undoubted services to the people and the country in defending the gains of the revolution. For a long time the state security organs justified this trust and their special status evoked no danger. The situation changed after Stalin's personal control over them had gradually superseded control by the party and the government, and the usual exercise of the standards of justice was not infrequently replaced by his individual decisions. The situation became still more aggravated when the criminal gang of the agent of international imperialism, Beria, got to the head of the state security organs. Serious violations of Soviet law and mass repressions then occurred. As a result of the machinations of our enemies, many honest Communists and non-party people had been slandered and suffered, although completely innocent.

The 20th Party Congress and the entire policy of the Central Committee after Stalin's death are vivid evidence of the fact that inside the Central Committee of the party there was a Leninist core of leaders who correctly understood the pressing needs in the spheres both of home and foreign policy. One cannot say that no counter-measures were taken against the negative phenomena that were associated with the cult of the individual and impeded the advance of socialism. Moreover, there were definite periods during the war, for example, when Stalin's individual actions were sharply restricted, when the negative consequences of lawlessness, arbitrariness, etc., were substantially reduced.

It is known that precisely during the war members of the Central Committee as well as outstanding Soviet military leaders took control of definite sections of activity in the rear and at the front, independently took decisions, and by their organisational, political, economic and military work, together with local party and government organisations, secured the victory of the Soviet people in the war. After the victory, the negative consequences of the cult of the individual again became strongly manifest.

Immediately after Stalin's death the Leninist core of the Central Committee took the path of vigorous struggle against the cult of the individual and its grave consequences.

The question may arise: Why then had these people not come out openly against Stalin and removed him from leadership? In the prevailing conditions this could not be done. The facts unquestionably show that Stalin was guilty of many unlawful acts that were committed, particularly in the last period of his life. However, one must not forget at the same time that the Soviet people knew Stalin as a man always acting in the defence of the USSR against the machinations of the enemies, and working for the cause of socialism. In this work he at times applied unseemly methods, and violated the Leninist principles and standards of party life. Herein was the tragedy of Stalin. And all this together made difficult the struggle against the lawless actions that were then being committed, because the successes in building socialism and strengthening the USSR were, in the atmosphere of the cult of the individual, ascribed to Stalin.

Any opposition to him under these circumstances would not have been understood by the people, and it was not at all a matter of lack of personal courage. It is clear that anyone who in these circumstances would have come out against Stalin would have got no support from the people. What is more, such opposition would have been evaluated, in those circumstances, as being against the cause of building socialism, as an extremely dangerous threat to the unity of the party and the whole state in conditions of capitalist encirclement. Moreover, the achievements of the working people of the Soviet Union under the leadership of the Communist Party instilled legitimate pride in the heart of every Soviet man and created an atmosphere in which individual errors and shortcomings seemed less important against the background of the tremendous achievements, and the negative consequences of these errors were rapidly compensated by the immensely growing vital forces of the party and Soviet society.

It should also be borne in mind that many facts about wrong actions of Stalin, particularly in the sphere of violating Soviet law, became known only lately, already after Stalin's death, chiefly in connection with the exposure of Beria's gang and the establishment of party control over the security organs.

Such are the chief conditions and reasons that resulted in the cult of J.V. Stalin's personality coming into being and spreading. All this, of course, explains, but by no means justifies, the cult of J.V. Stalin's personality and its consequences which have been so sharply and justly condemned by our party.

III

The cult of the individual, unquestionably, did grave harm to the cause of the Communist Party, to Soviet society. But it would be a great mistake to draw conclusions about some changes having taken place in the social system of the USSR from the fact that in the past there was the cult of the individual, or to see a source of this cult in the nature of the Soviet social system. Both conclusions are utterly wrong, as this is not in accordance with reality and is contrary to the facts.

Notwithstanding all the evil done to the party and the people by the cult of Stalin's personality, he could not, and did not change the nature of our social system. No cult of the individual could change the nature of the socialist state, which is based on social ownership of the means of production, the alliance of the working class and the peasantry, and friendship between the peoples, although this cult did cause serious harm to the development of socialist democracy and the promotion of the creative initiative of millions of people.

To think that one personality, even such a great one as Stalin, could change our social and political system is to lapse into profound contradiction with the facts, with Marxism, with truth, is to lapse into idealism. This would mean ascribing to an individual such excessive, supernatural powers as the ability to change a system of society and, moreover, such a social system in which the many-million strong masses of the working people are the decisive force.

As is known, the nature of a social and political system is determined by its mode of production, by who owns the means of production in society, by which class wields political power. The whole world knows that in our country, as a result of the October

Revolution and the triumph of socialism, a socialist mode of production has been established, that it is now already almost 40 years that power has belonged to the working class and the peasantry. Thanks to this the social system is growing stronger from year to year, and its productive forces are growing. Even our will-wishers cannot fail to recognise this fact.

The cult of the individual, as is known, resulted in some serious errors being made in the direction of various branches of activity of the party and the Soviet state, both in the domestic life of the Soviet Union and in its foreign policy. Among other things, one can point out serious errors committed by Stalin in the direction of agriculture, in organising the country's preparedness to rebuff the fascist invaders, and gross arbitrariness that led to the conflict in the relations with Yugoslavia in the postwar period. These errors harmed the development of individual aspects of the life of the Soviet state, and especially, in the last years of J.V. Stalin's life, impaired the development of Soviet society, but, naturally, did not divert it from the correct road of advancement to Communism.

Our enemies allege that the cult of Stalin's personality was engendered not by definite historical conditions that have now lapsed into the past, but by the Soviet system itself, by, in their opinion, its undemocratic nature, etc. Such slanderous assertions are refuted by the entire history of the development of the Soviet state. The Soviets as a new democratic form of state power came into being as a result of the revolutionary creative activity of the broadest masses of the people who rose in struggle for freedom. They have been and remain organs of genuine people's power. It is precisely the Soviet system that has made it possible to tap the tremendous creative energy of the people. It brought into motion inexhaustible forces inherent in the masses of the people, drew millions of people into conscientious administration of the state into active, creative participation in the construction of socialism. In a brief historical period, the Soviet state emerged victorious from the severest trials, stood the test in the fire of the Second World War.

When the last exploiting classes were eliminated in our country, when socialism became the dominant system in the entire national economy, and the international position of our country altered fundamentally, the bounds of Soviet democracy expanded immeasurably and are continuing to expand. In contrast to any bourgeois democracy, Soviet democracy not only proclaims but materially ensures all members of society without exception the right to work, education, rest and recreation, to participation in state affairs, freedom of speech, press and conscience, a real possibility for the free development of personal abilities, and all other democratic rights and freedoms. The essence of democracy lies not in formal signs but in whether the political power serves and reflects the will and fundamental interests of the majority of the people, the interests of the working folk. The entire domestic and foreign policy of the Soviet state shows that our system is a genuinely democratic, genuinely people's system. The supreme aim and daily concern of the Soviet state is the utmost advancement of the living standards of the population, the ensuring of a peaceful existence for its people.

Evidence of the further development of Soviet democracy is the measures that are being carried out by the party and the government for broadening the rights and competence of the Union republics, the strict observance of the law, reconstruction of the planning system with a view to unleashing local initiative, activizing the work of the local Soviets, developing criticism and self-criticism.

Notwithstanding the cult of the individual and in spite of it, the mighty initiative of the masses of the people, led by the Communist Party, initiative brought into being by our system, pursued its great historical task, overcoming all obstacles on the road to the construction of socialism. And herein lies the highest expression of the democracy of the Soviet socialist system. The outstanding victories of socialism in our country did not come by themselves. They were achieved by the tremendous organizational and educational work of the party and its local organizations, by the fact that the party always educated its cadres and all Communists in the spirit of loyalty to Marxism-Leninism, in the spirit of devotion to the cause of Communism. Soviet society is strong by the consciousness of the masses of the people. Its historical destinies have been and are determined by the constructive labour of our heroic working class, glorious collective farm peasantry, and people's intelligentsia.

Eliminating the consequences of the cult of the individual, re-establishing the Bolshevik standards of party life, developing socialist democracy, our party has further strengthened its ties with the broad masses of the people and has rallied them still closer under the great banner of Lenin.

The fact that the party itself has boldly and openly raised the question of eliminating the cult of the individual, of the impermissible errors committed by Stalin, is convincing proof that the party firmly guards Leninism, the cause of socialism and Communism, the observance of socialist law, the interests of the peoples and the rights of all Soviet citizens. This is the best proof of the strength and viability of the Soviet socialist system. At the same time it shows a determination finally to overcome the consequences of the cult of the individual and to prevent the recurrence of such errors in the future.

The condemnation of the cult of J.V. Stalin and its consequences has evoked endorsement and a broad response in all fraternal Communist and workers' parties. Noting the tremendous significance of the 20th Congress of the CPSU for the entire international Communist and labour movement, the Communists in the foreign countries regard the struggle against the cult of the individual and its consequences as a struggle for the purity of the principles of Marxism-Leninism, for a creative approach to the current problems of the international labour movement, for the consolidation and further development of the principles of proletarian internationalism.

Statements by a number of fraternal Communist parties express endorsement and support for the measures taken by our party against the cult of the individual and its consequences. Summarising the conclusions to be drawn from the discussion of the decisions of the 20th Congress of the CPSU by the Political Bureau of the Central Committee of the Communist Party of China, the party's newspaper *Jenminjihpao*, in an editorial "On the historical experience of the dictatorship of the proletariat", wrote:

"The Communist Party of the Soviet Union, following Lenin's behests, seriously regards some grave errors committed by Stalin in the direction of socialist construction, and their consequences. The graveness of these consequences raised before the Communist Party of the Soviet Union the necessity, simultaneously with recognizing Stalin's great services, of laying bare most sharply the essence of the errors committed by Stalin, and calling upon the entire party to take care to prevent a repetition of this, and to root out vigorously the unhealthy consequences of these errors. We, Chinese Communists, profoundly believe that after the sharp criticism that was displayed at the 20th Congress of the CPSU, all the active factors that were strongly restrained in the past because of certain political errors, will surely come into motion everywhere, that the Communist Party of the Soviet Union and the Soviet people will be still more united and rallied than before in the struggle for the construction of a great Communist society, unprecedented in the history of mankind, for lasting world peace."

"The merit of the leaders of the Communist Party of the Soviet Union," a statement of the Political Bureau of the French Communist Party says, "is the fact that they have undertaken to correct the errors and shortcomings associated with the cult of the individual, which testifies to the strength and unity of the great party of Lenin and the trust it enjoys among the Soviet people and to its prestige in the international movement." The General Secretary of the National Committee of the United States Communist Party, Comrade Eugene Dennis, noting the great significance of the 20th Congress of the CPSU, says in his well-known article: "The 20th Congress strengthened world peace and social progress. It marked a new stage in the advancement of socialism and in the struggle for peaceful coexistence that began in Lenin's day, continued in the following years, and is becoming ever more effective and successful."

At the same time it should be noted that in discussing the question of the cult of the individual, the causes of the cult of the individual and its consequences for our social system are not always correctly interpreted. Thus, for example, Comrade Togliatti's comprehensive and interesting interview given to the magazine *Nuovi Argomenti*, along with many quite important and correct conclusions, contains also wrong propositions. Particularly, one cannot agree with Comrade Togliatti's putting the question of whether Soviet society has not arrived at "certain forms of degeneration". There are no grounds for putting such a question. It is all the more incomprehensible in that in another part of his interview Comrade Togliatti quite correctly says: "It is necessary to draw the conclusion that the essence of the socialist system was not lost, just as not a single one of the previous gains was lost, and above all the support of the system by the masses of the workers, peasants and intelligentsia who make up Soviet society was not lost. This very support shows that, notwithstanding everything, this society has preserved its basic democratic nature."

Indeed, without the support of the broadest masses of the people for the Soviet government and the policy of the Communist Party, our country could not have built up in an unprecedentedly brief period a mighty socialist industry and effected the collectivization of agriculture, it could not have won the Second World War, on the outcome of which the destinies of all mankind depended. As a result of the utter rout of Hitlerism, Italian fascism and Japanese militarism, the forces of the Communist movement have broadly developed, the Communist Parties of Italy, France and other capitalist countries have grown and become mass parties, the people's democratic system has been established in a number of European and Asian countries, the world system of socialism has arisen and become consolidated, the national liberation movement, which has brought about the disintegration of the colonial system of imperialism, has scored unprecedented successes.

IV

Unanimously approving the decisions of the 20th Congress of the CPSU, which condemn the cult of the individual, the Communists and all Soviet people see in them evidence of the growing power of our party, of the strength of its Leninist principles, unity and solidarity. "The party of the revolutionary proletariat," V.I. Lenin pointed out, "is sufficiently strong to openly criticise itself, to call a mistake a mistake, and a weakness a weakness." (*Works*, Vol. 21, p. 150.) Guided by this Leninist principle, our party will continue, in future too, boldly to disclose, openly to criticise, and resolutely to eliminate mistakes and blunders in its work.

The Central Committee of the CPSU considers that the work accomplished by the party so far in overcoming the cult of the individual and its consequences has already yielded positive results.

On the basis of the decisions of the 20th Congress of the party, the Central Committee of the CPSU calls upon all party organisations:

Consistently to adhere in all their work to the most important principles of the teaching of Marxism-Leninism about the people being the makers of history, the creators of all the material and spiritual riches of mankind, on the decisive role of the Marxist party in the revolutionary struggle for the transformation of society, for the victory of Communism;

Persistently to continue the work, conducted in recent years by the Central Committee of the party, for the strictest observation by all party organisations, from top to bottom, of the Leninist principles of party leadership, and primarily of the supreme principle of collective leadership, the observation of the norms of party life, as fixed by the rules of the party, of developing criticism and self-criticsm;

Fully to restore the principles of Soviet socialist democracy as laid down in the Constitution of the Soviet Union finally to correct the violations of revolutionary socialist laws;

To mobilise our cadres, all Communists and the broadest masses of the working people, in the struggle for the practical realization of the targets of the sixth Five-Year Plan, giving the utmost stimulation to the creative initiative and energy of the masses, the true makers of history, in achieving this end.

The 20th Congress of the CPSU pointed out that the most important feature of our epoch is the conversion of socialiam into a world system. The most difficult period in the development and consolidation of socialism now lies behind us. Our socialist country has ceased to be a lonely island in an ocean of capitalist states. Today more than one-third of humanity is building a new life under the banner of socialism. The ideas of socialism are winning the support of many, many millions of people in the capitalist countries. The influence of the ideas of socialism is tremendous among the peoples of Asia, Africa and Latin America, who are fighting against all forms of colonialism.

The decisions of the 20th Congress of the CPSU are regarded by all supporters of peace and socialism, by all democratic and progressive circles, as an inspiring programme of struggle for the consolidation of peace throughout the world, for the interests of the working class, for the triumph of the cause of socialism.

Under present conditions, the Communist parties and the whole international labour movement are faced with broad, inspiring prospects — to secure, hand in hand with all the peaceful forces, the prevention of a new world war, to curb the monopolies and ensure lasting peace and the security of the peoples, to put an end to the armaments race and remove from the working peoples the heavy burden of taxes bred by it, to fight for the preservation of the democratic rights and liberties which facilitate the working people's struggle for a better life and a bright future. This is what the millions of ordinary people in every country of the world are vitally interested in. The successful solution of these problems is to a tremendous degree facilitated by the peaceful policy and the ever new successes of the Soviet Union, the Chinese People's Republic and all the other countries advancing on the road of socialism.

In the new historical conditions, such international organizations of the working class as the Comintern and the Cominform have ceased their activities. But this in no way means international solidarity has lost its significance and that there is no longer any need for contacts among the fraternal revolutionary parties adhering to the positions of Marxism-Leninism. At the present time, when the forces of socialism and the influence of socialist ideas have immeasurably grown throughout the world, when different means of achieving socialism in the various countries are being revealed, the Marxist working-class parties must naturally preserve and consolidate their ideological unity and fraternal international solidarity in the fight against the threat of a new war, in the fight against the anti-national forces of monopoly capital striving to suppress all the revolutionary and progressive movements. The Communist parties are welded together by the great objective of freeing the working class from the yoke of capital, they are united by their fidelity to the scientific ideology of Marxism-Leninism, to the spirit of proletarian internationalism, by the utmost devotion to the interests of the people.

In their activity under modern conditions, all the Communist parties base themselves on the national peculiarities and conditions of every country, giving the fullest expression to the national interests of their peoples. At the same time, recognizing that the struggle for the interests of the working class, for peace and the national independence of their countries is the cause of the entire international proletariat, they are consolidating their ranks and strengthening their contacts and co-operation among themselves. The ideological consolidation and fraternal solidarity of the Marxist parties of the working class in different countries are the more necessary since the capitalist monopolies are creating their own aggressive international coalitions and blocs, such as NATO, SEATO, and the Baghdad Pact, which are directed against the peace-loving peoples, against the national liberation movement, against the working class and the vital interests of the working peoples.

While the Soviet Union is continuing to do very much to bring about a relaxation in international tension — and this is now recognised everywhere — American monopoly capital continues to assign large sums of money for increasing the subversive activities in the socialist countries. When the cold war was at its height, the United States Congress, as is well known, officially appropriated (apart from the funds used unofficially) 100 million dollars for the purposes of conducting subversive activities in the people's democracies and the Soviet Union. Now that the Soviet Union and the other socialist countries are doing everything possible to ease international tension, the cold war adherents are seeking once more to galvanize the cold war, which has been condemned by the peoples of the entire world. This is shown by the decision of the United States Senate to appropriate an additional 25 million dollars for subversive activity, under the cynical pretext of "stimulating freedom" behind the "iron curtain".

We must soberly appraise this fact and draw the necessary conclusions from it. It is clear, for instance, that the anti-popular riots in Poznan have been paid for from this source. But the *agents-provocateurs* and subversive elements who were paid out of the overseas funds had enough "go" in them only for a few hours. The working people of Poznan resisted the hostile actions and provocations. The plans of the dark knights of the "cloak and dagger" have fallen through, their dastardly provocation against the people's power in Poland has failed. All future attempts at subversive actions in the people's democracies are similarly doomed to failure, even though such actions are generously paid for out of funds assigned by the American monopolies. This money may be said to be spent in vain.

All this shows that we must not allow ourselves to be indifferent about the new designs of the imperialist agencies, seeking to penetrate into the socialist countries in order to do harm and disrupt the achievements of the working people.

The forces of imperialist reaction are seeking to divert the working people from the true road of struggle for their interests, to poison their minds with disbelief in the success of the cause of peace and socialism. In spite of all the designs of the ideologists of the capitalist monopolies, the working class, headed by its tried Communist vanguard, will follow its own road, which has already led to the historic conquests of socialism, and will lead to new victories in the cause of peace, democracy and socialism. There can be no doubt that the Communist and Workers' parties of all countries will raise still higher the glorious Marxist banner of proletarian internationalism.

The Soviet people are naturally proud of the fact that our homeland was the first to pave the road to socialism. Now that socialism has become a world system, now that fraternal co-operation and mutual aid have been established among the socialist countries, new favourable conditions have been created for the flourishing of socialist democracy, for the further consolidation of the material and industrial basis of Communism, for a steady rise in the living standards of the working people, for an all-sided development of the personality of the new man, the builder of Communist society. Let the bourgeois ideologists invent fables about a "crisis" of Communism, about "dismay" in the ranks of the Communist parties. It is not the first time that we have heard incantations from enemies. All their predictions have always burst like bubbles. These sorry soothsayers have appeared and disappeared, while the Communist movement, the immortal and inspiring ideas of Marxism-Leninism, have advanced from victory to victory. So it will be in the future, too. No malicious, slanderous outburst of our enemies can stop the invincible, historic march of mankind towards Communism.